Bridging Atlantic Waters

A Commercial and Genealogical History of the Henleys of Devon and Newfoundland And Labrador 1538-2008.

John Carrick Greene

Triumphant Explorations Limited
St. John's NL 2008
www.trexplim.com

Printed in Quebec

Library and Archives Canada Cataloguing in Publication

Greene, John Carrick, 1939-
    Bridging Atlantic Waters: a commercial and genealogical history of the Henleys of Devon and Newfoundland/Labrador, 1538-2008 / John Carrick Greene.

Includes bibliographical references and index.
ISBN 978-0-9732059-1-6

    1. **Henley family. 2. Newfoundland and Labrador--Genealogy. 3. Devon (England)--Genealogy. 4. Newfoundland and Labrador--Commerce-- England—Devon History. 5. Devon (England)--Commerce--Newfoundland and Labrador--History. I. Title.**

CS90.H4552 2008   929'.20971   C2008 906371-3

Canada

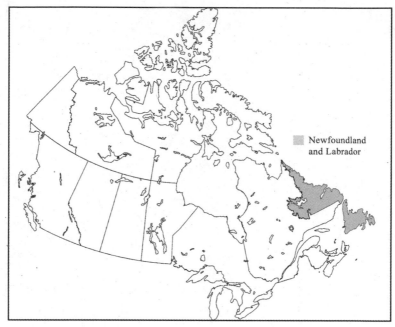

Newfoundland
and Labrador

Sources: 2001 Census of Canada. Base map: © 2000. Government of Canada with permission from Natural Resources Canada.
Produced by the Geography Division, Statistics Canada. © Minister of Industry, 2002. All Rights reserved.

 Statistics   Statistique
Canada   Canada

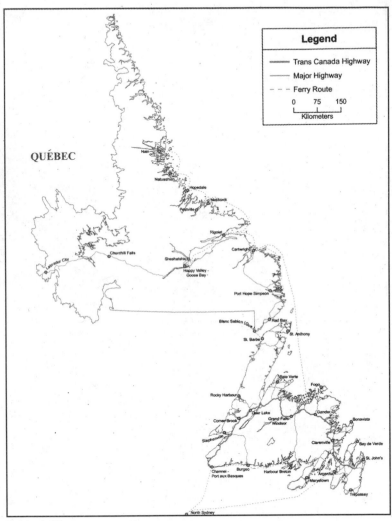

Department of Finance
Newfoundland and Labrador Statistics Agency

Map of Labrador (Southern Half)

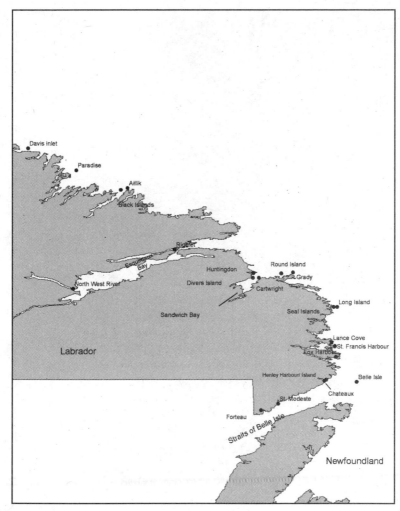

Created using ArcGIS 9.2 by Jennifer Fowler (2007)
Map Library, Memorial University of Newfoundland

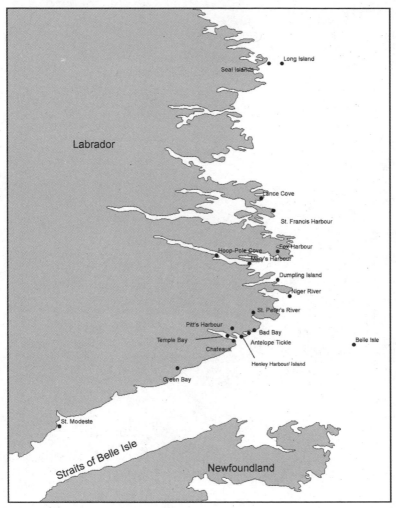

Long Island
Seal Islands
Labrador
Lance Cove
St. Francis Harbour
Fox Harbour
Hoop-Pole Cove
Mary's Harbour
Dumpling Island
Niger River
St. Peter's River
Pitt's Harbour
Bad Bay
Temple Bay
Antelope Tickle
Chateaux
Belle Isle
Henley Harbour/ Island
Green Bay
St. Modeste
Straits of Belle Isle
Newfoundland

Created using ArcGIS 9.2 by Jennifer Fowler (2007)
Map Library, Memorial University of Newfoundland

Map of Devon

Abbreviations

C O	Colonial Office
DCB	Dictionary of Canadian Biography
CNS	Center for Newfoundland Studies
DRO	Devon Record Office
FPU	Fishermen's Protective Union
HBC	Hudson's Bay Company
IGI	International Genealogical Index
LAC	Library and Archives Canada
LDS	Latter Day saints
LTA	Land Tax Assessments
MHA	Maritime History Archives
MNF	Matthews Name Files
PANL	Provincial Archives of Newfoundland and Labrador
QEII	Queen Elizabeth II Library
RAF	Royal Air Force
TNA	The National Archives, Kew, England.
WO	War Office

X

Table of Contents

Maps III

Abbreviations IX

Preface 1

Introduction 5

Part I: Commercial Endeavors

1 The West of England Newfoundland
  Fisheries 18

2 Henleys in the Avalon Fisheries 33

3 The Labrador Fisheries 39

4 The Henleys in Labrador 53

5 Making a Living in Devon 68

6 Modern Manufacturing in St. John's 80

Part II: Genealogy

1 Introduction 91

2 The Newton Abbot Henleys 101

3 The Dartmouth Henleys 125

4 The Torquay Henleys 135

5 The Newfoundland Henleys 150

6 Postscript 163

7 Family Tree 166

  Bibliography 208

  Index 225

Preface

In my youth I was continually aware of the history of the origins of the Henleys in Newfoundland and Labrador.

In the first instance it often seemed to me that some of the history was manufactured and I shouldn't be blamed for thinking such as my dad was a great tease and a bit of a character. Quite often in my young mind I couldn't distinguish facts from fiction.

As I got older, however, oral history enunciated certain details that evoked within me a curiosity of the Henley origins in Newfoundland and Labrador.

I was aware of Henley Harbour and its recorded ties to our family but the stories lacked detail and I was unaware of the genealogical facts.

After the death of my Dad in 1942 I became more curious and endeavored to research, in my own amateur genealogical fashion, the origins of the Henley family in this province.

For a period of years I attempted to trace names and their relationship to the Henley family, but I had great difficulty. I had a problem with my eyesight for as I began to review the numerous microfilm reels in the Archives I would become somewhat "cross-eyed" as it were, and quite often suffered either a severe headache or an apparent bout of 'sea-sickness'. Thus my effort was diminished to a great extent and I became discouraged by the immensity of the task.

In the last number of years, however, I decided to seek some professional help on this project and, following consultations with family and fiends, I selected the historian and genealogist John Carrick Greene.

I had become fascinated with his excellent book **Between Damnation And Starvation** and was very much impressed with his genealogical work, **Of Fish And Family**. I, therefore, commissioned him on a fee-for-service basis to undertake research on the Henley origins in Newfoundland and Labrador.

I was not to be disappointed. I have found John's scholarship in this field to be exceptional and his attention to detail remarkable.

As a result of his commission John reported to me regularly, giving specific reports to date and on each and every occasion I was led to see a much clearer picture of the Henley story. But it was far more concrete and detailed than I had ever imagined.

I was aware for example of the old Henley Rooms on the St. John's waterfront. They had been identified by an amateur genealogist, the late Doug Muir, of Muir's Marble Works. I was also aware of the background of my great-grand-father and my great-great-grand-father, and their reputed connections with Henley Harbour, but concrete evidence was lacking. My late Aunt (Min) Cahill helped me locate certain Henley graves in Belvedere cemetery. On one Sunday morning just before she died she gave me some indications as to where my great grandfather's grave could be found. Up to that time I had invested considerable time in the old part of the cemetery looking for the grave without success. With Aunt Min's advice I was eventually able to locate the grave of my late great-grand-father, James, whose stone also carried the name of his daughter, Elisa, buried in the same plot. Next to his headstone stood the memorial of his sister, Mary, who had married Captain Stafford. Those discoveries further stimulated my interest in piecing together our family history.

John Greene's work has not only uncovered the genealogical facts of our family history but has provided me with a huge background on our family's commercial history, as well as that of Newfoundland and Labrador at the same time. Based upon his efforts and extensive research I have nothing but praise for his thoroughness and scholarship in the fields of genealogy and history. His contacts and explorations in Devon and the relations he has recounted concerning Henley Harbour and the Labrador trade have opened my eyes to facts that were unknown to me.

As a result, thereof, of the information unearthed by John's research I elected, with two of my children, to visit Henley Harbour. Thus, I flew into Mary's Harbour, hired a longliner and spent two days exploring the plantations where my ancestors fished so long, long ago. It was an emotional and rewarding experience to sit on the stool of the properties originally created by my ancestors, properties now owned by the Stone family in that harbour.

My emotions were further touched as I began to receive more and more results from John. About a year and a half ago I agreed with his suggestion to produce a book out of this research and to write and publish it on his own responsibility. This book is therefore the end result of years of research on our family history. I never imagined that he would uncover such an illuminating story of our family's commercial dealings and genealogical undertakings. I remain fascinated with his approach to the subject and with the information his research has yielded. I feel certain that this book represents a significant contribution to the

commercial history of this province and to
the county of Devon in the old country. I
compliment John Greene for his remarkable
efforts and without being considered
egotistical in any sense I strongly recommend
this book as an excellent read.

Alec G Henley
St. John's.

Introduction

The Henleys have compiled an extensive business history on both sides of the Atlantic Ocean. In Devon, where they originated and in Newfoundland And Labrador, to which some of them emigrated in the eighteenth century, they carried on business in trade and manufacturing. This study seeks to present as clear a portrait as possible of the several Henley firms on both sides of the Atlantic Ocean by viewing the external experiences of their various commercial interests. It will conclude with a genealogical study of the Henley families of both Newfoundland and Devon.

Back in Devon their business interests, until the 1790's, centered almost entirely on the Newfoundland fisheries. From Newton Abbot, Torquay and Dartmouth those 18th century Henleys acquired interests in shipping and engaged in the carrying trade to Newfoundland And Labrador. At the same time they established fisheries on their own account with hired servants and shipping crews criss-crossing the Atlantic Ocean until economic transformations wiped out the migratory fishery in the nineteenth century.

Although Henley crossings to Newfoundland had ceased by 1825 it did not mean a total withdrawal from business on the part of the Henleys. For on the Avalon Peninsula, in Labrador and in Devon, the Henleys continued their commercial ventures.

In Devon they continued primarily in the construction trades in Dartmouth and Torquay except for those in the Newton Abbot-Abbotskerswell area. There the Henleys, before the eighteenth century had closed, embarked on a path of manufacturing that eventually led to their making a national

name for themselves in the production of
fruit liquors. And they remained in that
sector until the 1930's.

On this side of the Atlantic Ocean they
were engaged in the cod, seal and salmon
fisheries on the Labrador coast down to the
last quarter of the nineteenth century. And
the opening years of the twentieth century
witnessed them entering the furniture and
mattress manufacturing sector in St. John's,
a venture that lasted until the mid-1950's.
Two hundred years of commercial endeavors
that spanned the Atlantic Ocean makes for an
interesting history but there are almost
insurmountable challenges that face the
historian in attempting to recreate that
history.

First of all there is the paucity of
secondary literature on the merchant families
of Newfoundland And Labrador as well as on
those who remained in Devon. It is a
distinguishing characteristic of Newfoundland
And Labrador historiography that our merchant
families and their enterprises have been
almost entirely neglected by our researchers.
The best literary productions, as well as the
most prominent in the field, have been the
works, in the one case, on a firm that was
largely involved on the mainland of Canada
and only marginally involved in Newfoundland
And Labrador and, in the other, dealt with a
fishermen's organization with substantial
holdings in the fishery.

In the first case there is the Hudson's
Bay Company that operated in Labrador from
the early part of the 19th century down to our
own time. A substantial quantity of
literature has been produced on that firm
both in the form of academic books as well as
scholarly journal articles. A search of
Memorial University Libraries, alone, turns
up three hundred and ninety-five titles.

However, one need only refer to Newman's work for an excellent comprehensive history of that organization.[1]

In the other case we must note the historically famous Fishermen's Protective Union founded in 1908 at Herring Neck and destined to become the largest producer and exporter of fish in the colony. Twenty-six titles are displayed in Memorial's Centre for Newfoundland Studies catalogue on that organization but almost all of them deal with the political activities of the FPU. Those interested in the business activities of that body should refer to Coaker, Hon Sir W F, ed, **Twenty Years of the Fishermen's Protective Union Of Newfoundland** (St. John's: Advocate Publishing Company, Ltd, 1930); Wanda Legge's and Robert Thompson's brief to the Royal Commission in 1986 is a useful study of co-ops and other Community Based Organization's in the fishery in the 1980's.[2] Unfortunately very few scholars have paid any attention to the private firms and Harris's **Rare Ambition**[3] broke new ground in this field as he chronicled the exploits of the famous Crosbie family through politics and business in the 19th and 20th centuries. While it is the only

---

[1]Newman, Peter C, **The Company of Adventurers** (Markham: Viking Press, 1985); students interested in furthering their studies on that company would do well to check out Newman's bibliography; those interested in the Labrador theatre of the company's work should consult McDonald, Donna, **Lord Strathcona: A Biography of Donald Alexander Smith** (Toronto: Dundurn Press, 2002); Smith spent twenty years working for the HBC on the Labrador coast in the middle years of the 19th century.

[2]Legge, Wanda and Thompson, Robert, "Community based organizations in the fish processing industry in Newfoundland and Labrador" (St. John's: Royal Commission on Employment and Unemployment, Newfoundland and Labrador, 1986).

[3]Harris, Michael, **Rare Ambition: The Crosbies Of Newfoundland** (Toronto: Penguin Books, 1993).

published, professional monograph produced to
date on Newfoundland's private entrepreneurs
there are several smaller offerings in the
form of booklets, leaflets, promotional
offerings, recollections, journalistic
accounts and others that the beginner should
consult. The firm, James Baird (Labrador) Ltd.
published a very short but extremely useful
sketch of its business activities on the
Labrador coast in the 1940's that contains
several pages of accounts.[4] Lucy Earle's study
of Baine Johnston & Co on the southern
Labrador coast of the 1940's is valuable for
the same reason.[5] Warwick Smith's five-page
sketch of A E Hickman Company Limited is
valuable for its dates, family names and
lists of the various sectors in which Hickman
was involved.[6] And David Keir's promotional
booklet on the Bowring company[7] does for that
firm what Smith did for Hickman's. Donald
Warr's paper on Newman's account books,[8]
although covering a brief, 10-year period,
contains valuable statistics on prices,
production volumes etc. But perhaps the most
valuable studies performed on private firms
in Newfoundland to date are those done by

---

[4]Snow, Edward A, **A company history and financial statement as of Dec, 31, 1949**, (St. John's: James Baird (Labrador) Ltd, 1950).
[5]Earle, Lucy M, "Like a cat would watch a rat : social and economic relationships between Baine, Johnston & Company Ltd., and the fishermen of the Battle Harbour district, 1940-1945" (Memorial University, Honors Dissertation, 2003).
[6]Smith, Warwick, "The tale of a fish merchant - The story of A.E. Hickman Company, Ltd" in *Newfoundland Magazine*, St. John's, December 1920, Vol. 4(3), 2-6.
[7]Keir, David, **The Bowring Story** (London: Bodley Head Ltd, 1962).
[8]Warr, Donald A, "A study of Newman's Company in Newfoundland from 1850-1859" (Memorial University: a paper presented to the Maritime History Group, 1973).

Chang[9], Mannion,[10] Macdonald[11], Thornton[12] and Bradley [13] . Chang's thesis was the first academic study of a private fish company in this province and is a must-read for the commercial historian. Mannion's excellent

---

[9]Chang, Margaret, "Newfoundland in Transition: the Newfoundland trade and Robert Newman and Company, 1780-1805" (St. John's: Memorial University, M A Thesis, 1974).

[10]Mannion, John, "Patrick Morris and Newfoundland Irish Immigration" in Byrne, Cyril and Harry, Margaret, eds, **Talamh an Eisc: Canadian and Irish Essays** (Halifax: Nimbus, 1986);

[11]Macdonald, David A, "They Cannot Pay Us in Money: Newman and Company and the Supplying System in the Newfoundland fishery, 1850-1884" in Ommer, Rosemary E, ed, **Merchant Credit and Labour Strategies in Historical Perspective** (Fredericton: Acadiensis Press, 1990); Ibid, "Really no merchant: an ethnohistorical account of Newman and Company and the supplying system in the Newfoundland fishery at Harbour Breton, 1850-1900" (Vancouver: Simon Fraser University, Ph D Thesis, , 1988); although Robert C H Sweeney's "Accounting For Change: Understanding Merchant Credit Strategies In Outport Newfoundland" in Candow, James E and Carol Corbin, eds, **How deep is the ocean? : historical essays on Canada's Atlantic fishery** (Sydney, N S : University College of Cape Breton Press, 1997) is an examination of but a three-year period yet it is one of the most scholarly examinations of fish company practices and deserves to be placed at the top of the commercial historian's reading list in this province.

[12]Thornton, Patricia, "The Transition from the Migratory to The Resident Fishery in the Strait of Belle Isle" in Ommer, 1990.

[13]Bradley, David Gordon, "Smugglers, Schemers, Scoundrels And Sleeveens: An Analysis of Merchant-Client Relations At Bonavista, Newfoundland, 1875-1895" (St. John's: Memorial University, M A Thesis, 1994); for more general studies of the mercantile community see Orr, J A, "Scottish Merchants in the Newfoundland Trade, 1800-1835: A Colonial Community in Transition" (St. John's: Memorial University, M A Thesis, 1987); Smith, Marjorie, "Newfoundland 1815-1840: A Study of Merchantocracy" (St. John's: Memorial University, M A Thesis, 1968); Sager, Eric, "The Merchants of Water Street and Capital Investment in Newfoundland's Traditional Economy" in Fischer, Lewis R and Eric Sager, eds, **The Enterprising Canadians: Entrepreneurs and Economic Development in Eastern Canada, 1820-1914** (St. John's: Maritime History Group, 1979).

article on one of Newfoundland's most famous merchants reveals the details of the passenger and provisions trade in the first half of the nineteenth century. McDonald's two very scholarly works were the first academic publications resulting from analyses of the internal operations of fishing firms in Newfoundland And Labrador. His conclusions, supported by the evidence, overturned traditional views of what was considered to be the typical Newfoundland fish merchant. Thornton's study of the account books of west-country merchant, Joseph Bird, appeared simultaneously with McDonald's and gave us the first insightful view of the actual transition from the migratory fishery to a settled way of life. Bradley disputed the traditional view of mercantile enslavement of fish catchers and revealed that fishermen, by adopting a variety of strategies, were able to exercise a considerable degree of independence.

As for Devon there are fewer productions in that county on the firms involved in the Newfoundland And Labrador trade than there are here. When, in 1992, an English university professor produced a scholarly article on the Devon-Newfoundland fisheries he could only instance one secondary work in that field from his side of the ocean.[14] When I visited Exeter University in 2006 I learned of a student who was attempting to do a Ph. D. thesis on the Devon Newfoundland/Labrador fisheries but who was hampered by the fact that so few secondary works had been written in England that could serve as an introductory background to the

---

[14]Starkey, David J "Devonians and the Newfoundland Trade" in Michael Duffy et al, eds, **The New Maritime History of Devon, vol. I** (London: Conway Maritime Press Ltd, 1992).

subject. In fact a bibliographical search
retrieved only one monographic work on
Devon/Newfoundland merchants.[15] In addition I
must note at least two theses in Devon on
related subjects that are helpful to the
historian of the Devon-Newfoundland trade.[16]

The lack of previous research or
secondary literature should not in themselves
deter an enterprising scholar from breaking
new ground in a particular subject area. But
when the very records of the firms themselves
are non-existent then it poses an
incomparable challenge. When I visited the
Devon Record Office in 2006 I was informed by
the chief archivist that not a single record
had survived from any of the business firms
trading to Newfoundland. Newfoundland's
record is not much better, for researching
the fishing history of this province poses a
singular challenge by virtue of the fact that
ninety-nine percent of the fishery firms that
pre-date 1892 left no records at all. Only
two firms of the eighteenth and nineteenth
century eras have left a continuous series of
records that allow an intelligent study of
their operations. In attempting to
reconstruct our fishery history from primary
sources historians must rely, solely, on

[15]Freeman, Ray, **The Contribution of the Holdsworth & Newman Families to Dartmouth** (Dartmouth: Dartmouth History Research Group, 1992); see also Born, Anne, **The Torbay Towns** (Chichester: Phillimore & Co Ltd, 1989) for helpful references to the Newfoundland trade.
[16]Niering, Francis Eduard, "Andrew Pinson: Dartmouth Merchant, ship owner and gentleman farmer trading to Labrador" (Exeter: University of Exeter, M A Thesis, 1999); Northway, A. M, "The Devon Fishing Industry 1760-1860" (Exeter: University of Exeter, M A Thesis, 1969); mention should also be made of the following: Davies, Glanville James, "England And Newfoundland: Policy and trade 1660-1783 (Southampton: University of Southampton, Ph D Thesis, 1980).

fragmentary evidence that has managed to survive from a variety of companies.

The main point which I wish to impress upon readers is that I have attempted to compile a history of commercial firms in Newfoundland and Labrador and Devon without the benefit of any surviving records of those firms in question. One must wonder then how it could be done at all and that requires further explanation.

First, it must be admitted that the actual internal operations of the firms in question could never really be known with certainty. For example, we can never be sure of the actual starting and ending dates of firms for whom no correspondence has survived. Nor can we be certain of the actual founder's name especially if it was a family concern originating in the 18th or early 19th century. It goes without saying that we can never know anything about the accounting practices or the financial state of the business at any particular time. The details of their purchasing policies must remain hidden and their sales and market specifics can only be inferred from the thin trail left by contemporary observers and fellow entrepreneurs.

What sources, then, can be used to reconstruct a commercial history? First of all we must follow a sparse trail through all the public records that have survived. In this province they include the various series of correspondence between the various Governors, the British government and other officials in this province. Those extensive files encompass the period from the seventeenth century down to the 1930's and are replete with fishery reports, statistics, petitions and merchant correspondence. Then there is an extensive file of newspapers, magazines, directories and almanacs covering

the period from 1805 down to our own time. In
Devon the public records include a series of
land records created by the land tax
collectors, commencing in the middle of the
18th century, that yield crucial information
on landholdings down to 1832. At the same
time they convey some illuminating
revelations on genealogy. There, also,
researchers will discover an even more
comprehensive file of newspapers, magazines,
directories and almanacs and, as in
Newfoundland, a small collection of archived
wills. I should also add that there is a
small collection of twentieth century
incorporation and bankruptcy documents at the
National Archives, Kew, England, on the
Henley Cider company that yielded some
important pieces of information on that
company's history. .

In the field of private records
priority of place must be given to the
records belonging to the Slade firm of Fogo
and those of the Newman-Hunt firm. The latter
operated mainly on the south coast, for over
two hundred years down to 1906. Although
their records yielded no information on the
firms forming the subject of this book no
commercial historian of this province can
ignore them for they constitute the best
evidence in existence regarding the fisheries
of olden days. What was more important for my
study were the numerous small files and
fragments that have survived from other fish
companies in Newfoundland And Labrador. They
range from a few sheets of accounts and
correspondence in some instances, to a one-
year ledger for others, or to spasmodic day
books and journals in other cases. All such
pieces yielded some clues on the Henley fish
firms of this book but the greatest source in
that category were the records of the
Hudson's Bay Company. That company was

involved throughout the 19th century all over
the Labrador coast and did a brisk business
with other firms there, especially with Hunt
and Henley. Their records are the most
impressive of all historical records I have
ever seen due to their enormous quantity and
unsurpassed quality. From 1670 down to recent
years they comprise almost four thousand
reels of microfilm and their legibility is
such that they could have been written
yesterday. The correspondence of the Trading
Post managers on the coast of Labrador
contains more valuable information on the
various fisheries than any individual
collection anywhere. And the Labrador
genealogist will be pleased to learn that
those managers faithfully recorded deaths,
sometimes births too, and frequently
performed marriages whose records they
dutifully preserved. Those records are all
located at the Manitoba Archives in Winnipeg
but microfilm copies are available at Library
And Archives Canada in Ottawa. The local
student will be delighted to learn that those
microfilms can be borrowed by means of inter-
library loan and can be viewed at your
regional library providing it has custody of
a microfilm reader.

Private records at the Devon Record
Office did not yield such fruitful results as
those in Newfoundland or Ottawa. Nevertheless
that institution possesses about 40,000 legal
documents which were acquired from various
legal firms over the years. The indentures
there contain every conceivable agreement
regarding land or property, such as sales and
purchases, leases, rents, transfers,
conveyances, abstracts of title etc. They
yielded to me several bundles in the shape of
parchment rolls on the Henley families of
Devon. Unfortunately only about 16,000 had
been indexed by the time I visited there in

2006 and the remainder retain their secrets in the form of parchment rolls many of which have remained unrolled for hundreds of years.

Naturally, in a quest of this nature where clues needed to be retrieved from a wide variety of sources the list of institutions and individuals to thank is rather lengthy. The number of personnel who rendered their very kind assistance is too lengthy to name individually and I must be content in naming the institutions only. They are as follows: in Canada: Provincial Archives of Newfoundland and Labrador, St. John's; Maritime History Archives, [17] St. John's; Queen Elizabeth II Library (their Archives and Manuscripts Division, especially the Centre for Newfoundland Studies), [18] St. John's; St. Thomas's Anglican Parish, St. John's; Anglican Cathedral Parish, St. John's; Basilica Roman Catholic Parish, St. John's; Roman Catholic Archdiocesan Archives, St. John's; Hudson's Bay Company Archives, Winnipeg; Library and Archives Canada, Ottawa; in England: Devon Record Office, Exeter; University of Exeter, Exeter; The Devon Family History Society, Exeter; Exeter Central Library, Exeter; Westcountry Studies Library, Exeter; Public Library, Torquay; Public Record Office, Kew; Museum of English Rural Life, University of Reading, Reading.

The personnel at QE II, especially those at CNS, MHA and the Map Library rendered such courteous, friendly and helpful service that they must be singled out for special praise. No personnel anywhere can surpass them in the quality of service they provide.

---

[17]Hereafter cited as MHA.
[18]Hereafter cited as CNS.

A significant number of individuals went beyond the call of duty in assisting my research. Some of them contributed precious pieces of information especially to the genealogy. They are as follows: in Canada: Allan Dwyer, St. John's; Terry Taylor, Oakville, ON and Edna Marlow, Ottawa; in England: Sally Heggie and Simon Wood at the Devon Family History Society, Exeter; Ian Stoyles, Exeter; Tom Jewell, Exeter; Arthur French, Ipplepen; Marion Giles, Plymouth; Terry Leaman and Mrs. J. Cooper, Torquay; Dorcas Mary Hester, East Molesey, Surrey; Janet Chapman, Kent; Elizabeth Howard, Norfolk; Anne Peat,Rickmansworth,Herts; in Australia: Ross Wilson in Brisbane; Lorraine Peach, Bob Reed, Robyn Way, Melbourne; Trudy Smith, Jan Bryant and Debbie Corder, Victoria; in the USA: P Scott Brown, Eureka, CA, Lesley Donald, Albany, WA; I would also like to thank the very valuable Devon-L list at http://genuki.cs.ncl.ac.uk for teaching me some very helpful lessons on Devon history and genealogy.

Most important of all I wish to thank Alec G Henley of St. John's who, in 2000, commissioned me on a professional basis to research his family's commercial and genealogical history. When it was completed in 2005 I suggested it would make a good book that was worth publishing. He subsequently accepted my proposal to write and publish this book on my own responsibility. I hope it will meet the approval of all Henley descendants on both sides of the Atlantic Ocean as well as meriting the approbation of the reading public.

Part I: Commercial Endeavors

Chapter I

The West of England Newfoundland
Fisheries

Every schoolboy knows that John Cabot discovered Newfoundland in 1497 for the King of England and in the following decades a prolific fishery developed featuring the ships and mariners of many nations. But what every schoolboy may not know was that, for the English, the Newfoundland fishery was just another fishery, as they had been involved in fishing nearer their own shores for centuries by the time Cabot announced his finding.

Fishing is of course as old as the human race, as early man responded to his desire for food by eating fish as well as wild animals. Even by the Middle Ages English fishermen were plying the North Sea for herrings and Icelandic waters for cod. In Devon, for example, the rich fishing grounds off the coast of the West Country were exploited well through medieval times and a small export trade had developed[1]. In the time of Richard II dried hake was exported from Exeter. Salmon was also an important fishery in Devon and appears in the records as early as the 9th century[2]. By 1378 pilchards and hake were among the principal articles of commerce for the port of Plymouth. Catching, salting and exporting them were the chief activities of Plymouth down to the late 18th century. In those days English armies were

---

[1]Hoskins, W. G, **A New Survey Of England Devon** (Newton Abbot: David & Charles, 1978), 212; for an excellent survey of the Devon-Newfoundland Fisheries see David J Starkey "Devonians and the Newfoundland Trade" in Michael Duffy et al.
[2]Ibid, 216.

fed on herring and one battle against the French in 1429 has gone down in history as "The Battle of Herrings". That was a result of an accidental encounter with the enemy by the English food convoy[3]. In fact herring was once so important that in 1532 Scotland and Holland went to war to solve a herring dispute which had developed off the coast of Scotland[4]. By that date Devon ports such as Exmouth, Tor Bay, Brixham and St. Marychurch were well known as fishing ports, ports later to be heavily involved in the Newfoundland trade.

Archaeologist and historian Peter Pope reports that the West Country experienced a rapid expansion in the fishing industry after 1400 that was fueled by an increased demand for fish in the home market[5]. Devon and Cornwall were the counties that figured chiefly in that expansion and although they had been involved for some time in both English Channel and Icelandic fisheries it was a new salt fish industry on the west coast of Ireland that figured mostly in the new boom. By the time economic and political conditions in Europe forced their attention on Cabot's new discovery West Countrymen had amassed all the expertise they needed for the catching, salting and drying of fish on the other side of the ocean.

One of the marked characteristics of the English fishing industry was the large quantity of fish imported, for there was a

[3]March, Edjar J, **Sailing Drifters: The Story of the Herring Luggers of England, Scotland and the Isle of Man** (London: Percival Marshall And Company Limited, 1952), 3.
[4]Ibid, 4.
[5]Pope, Peter E, **Fish into Wine: The Newfoundland Plantation In The Seventeenth Century** (Chapel Hill: University of North Carolina Press, 2004), 11-12.

considerable import trade with the continent[6]. Herrings, for example, were imported from the Netherlands and the Baltic states. But even more crucial was the fact that this import trade was dominated by foreign shipping, especially Dutch and Flemish. Only half the ships using the port of Hull in the 15th century were English ships. The remainder belonged to the Low Countries. This becomes of crucial significance later in the 16th century[7].

By the late 15th century England had possessed a long history of fishing and whatever catch domestic fishermen could not supply for the home market was satisfied by continental imports. Thus the English paid little attention to Cabot's discovery of new fisheries, for their demands were already being satisfied in the various ways described above. However, throughout the early 16th century English fishing ships began to find their way to Newfoundland, although in very small numbers. But it wasn't until well into the second half of that century that the Newfoundland fisheries acquired a status of any importance to the English nation[8].

---

[6]Bolton, J. L, **The Medieval English Economy 1150-1500** (London: J M Dent & Sons Ltd, 1980), 276; see also Peter King, **The Development of the English Economy To 1750** (London: Macdonald & Evans Ltd, 1971).

[7]Below, 22-3.

[8]The most authoritative and detailed study of those fisheries is Keith Matthews, "A History of the West of England-Newfoundland Fishery" (Oxford: University of Oxford, Ph. D thesis, 1968); see also Gillian T Cell, **English Enterprise in Newfoundland 1577-1660** (Toronto: University of Toronto Press, 1969); C. Grant Head, **Eighteenth-Century Newfoundland** (Toronto: McClelland and Stewart 1976); Harold A Innis, **The Cod Fisheries: The History of an International Economy** (Toronto: University of Toronto Press, 1978); Ralph G. Lounsbury, **The British Fishery at Newfoundland 1634-1763**(New Haven, n.p. 1934); Patrick O'Flaherty, **Old Newfoundland: A History**

The great Newfoundland historian, D W Prowse, claims that the first English ship to fish at Newfoundland began operations in 1498[9] but he gives no source for that historic event. Prowse declares further that to our forefathers in the time of Henry VII (1485-1509) "...the discovery of the fishing grounds of Newfoundland was a veritable God-send-a piscatorial El-Dorado."[10] Modern professional research has not been able to establish the truth of that claim either. Instead the efforts of modern scholars have refuted Prowse's claims. Gillian Cell has shown that even by the 1570's the English fishing fleet at Newfoundland numbered a mere four ships[11] and that only in the decades following 1577 did the English fleet grow to significant proportions. This growth occurred as a result of changing economic and political conditions on the international scene.

First, there were the numerous wars that plagued England in the last half of the 16th century. Henry VIII took England to war against Scotland and France in 1542 and by the time he died five years later it was still unresolved. Most of the next decade under Elizabeth was spent fighting France and in the early 1560's she involved England in the religious wars there and in Scotland. From 1585 to the end of her reign England was continually at war with Spain.

For many years preceding those wars there were the usual preparations in case of

to **1843** (St. John's: Long Beach Press, 1999); Pope, **Fish into Wine;** The best study of the nineteenth –century cod-fishery is Shannon Ryan, **Fish out of Water: The Newfoundland Saltfish Trade, 1814-1914** (St. John's: Breakwater Books 1986).
[9]Prowse, D. W, **History of Newfoundland, 3rd edn.** (St. John's: Dicks And Company Limited, 1971), 17.
[10]Ibid, 18.
[11]Cell, 22.

open hostilities so that England could be said to be on a war footing for an extended period of time. The contemplation of invasions by sea forced the English leaders to consider as to how best to provide the ships and train the mariners requisite for such an eventuality. In the 1560's Queen Elizabeth's Secretary, William Cecil, argued for an expansion of fish consumption to serve both those purposes[12]. We must remember that the carrying trade up to Cecil's time had been dominated by foreigners. Accordingly in 1563 he sponsored a Commons Bill that increased the number of fish days from one to two a week and permitted the custom-free export of fish in English-owned vessels. By the first provision he intended to expand the home market and the object of the second was to give control of the carrying trade to native merchants. That did not necessarily mean a big boost to the Newfoundland fisheries, however, for the chief sources of England's cod remained the bountiful waters off Iceland and Ireland. But Denmark had recently reinforced her hold on Iceland to the great disadvantage of England and then in 1580 began to exact license fees that seriously annoyed the English fishermen. That may have been the shot-in-the-arm required by the Newfoundland fisheries, for a sharp expansion in English activity in Newfoundland occurred almost immediately. In 1580 only fifty to sixty English ships were fishing at Newfoundland. But by 1599 at least twenty-six ships from the port of Dartmouth, alone, were frequenting Newfoundland and by 1610 the English fishing fleet at Newfoundland had grown to two-hundred. Pope gives alternative explanations for the dramatic expansion of

---

[12]Cell, 23.

England's activities in Newfoundland [13] . He
says that England's main competitors in the
salt fish markets of southern Europe were
suffering serious setbacks as a result of a
variety of domestic and foreign policy
reversals. As a result the center of the
European economy shifted from the
Mediterranean to the North Sea. English
fishermen, with their long experience and
advantages offered by the geographical
locations of their excellent ports, were well
placed to exploit the new opportunities. But
whatever the real reasons we know that a
marked expansion of the West Country
fisheries at Newfoundland occurred in the
first quarter of the 17th century. Thus there
began to blossom the internationally famous
West of England-Newfoundland fisheries that
drew the attention of governments on both
sides of the Atlantic Ocean until the last
west-country firm closed its doors in
Newfoundland in 1906.

Traditionally the counties of Devon,
Dorset, Somerset and Hampshire assumed
leading roles in the exploitation of the
Newfoundland fisheries. They were well placed
to capitalize on those opportunities. First,
they were the closest of the English ports to
the new world and had a long established
fishing history by the time of Cabot's
discovery. But most important of all was
their possession of coastline indented with
numerous, commodious and beautifully
sheltered, harbours offering tantalizing
invitations to the sea-going entrepreneur.
The people of those harbours and their
hinterlands took to the Newfoundland
fisheries as a natural expression of their
talents and material advantages. By the
early 17th century they had developed a series

---

[13]Pope, 17-9.

of complex relationships with Newfoundland. Matthews, Cell and Pope have supplied us with a wealth of detail related to the actual operations of those hardy fishers.

In December of each year the West Country fishermen began preparations for their annual migrations to Newfoundland. They tended their boats with all necessary repairs, then planned and purchased the provisions needed for the approximately six months away from home. Throughout the winter months they hired their crews and in March or April sailed for Newfoundland harbours. In May and June they prepared their stages, flakes, cookrooms, and whatever other buildings were required for the prosecution of the fishery from May to September. Then, having dried the salted fish, they sailed for their home ports or the markets of the continent.

Once in Newfoundland the English were forced to carry on a fishery quite different from that of the continental Europeans. The French, Spanish, Portuguese etc. carried on a 'wet' fishery by which is meant that they carried their fish back to Europe in its 'wet' or 'green', uncured state. They were able to perform that kind of operation because they had a plentiful supply of salt to properly preserve their fish for the long periods in which they were engaged in loading their schooners and/or sailing back across the ocean. The English, however, had no domestic supplies of salt and had to purchase it from their competitors on the continent. They therefore gravitated to a dry fishery which required a small amount of salt. It is common knowledge in a fishing country like Newfoundland that a dry fishery demands a light salted cure and that the wet or green fishery is frequently designated by Newfoundlanders as "heavy salted". Perhaps that is the reason we so readily accepted the

standard but simple explanation as to the
origins of the English dry fishery. In fact
the effect of the English dependence on
foreign supplies of salt has taken on the
proportions of a myth, a myth however that
Peter Pope has recently exploded[14]. Pope has
shown that it was the markets for the English
product that really determined the type of
fishery, for the people who consumed English
fish had a preference for a light salted cure.
And that, of course, is a phenomenon to which
a veteran Newfoundland fishing family can
easily relate.

The dry fishery, of course, meant that
the fish had to be caught near the land-based
operations and therefore the English dry
fishery became an inshore as opposed to an
offshore, fishery. But salting and drying
fish on shore also demanded shore space and
for that reason England insisted on claiming
Newfoundland as her own. By 1583 it was found
necessary to send out Sir Humphrey Gilbert to
announce formal possession and warn all
foreigners to keep their hands off England's
new overseas possession.

Matthews reports that up to 1570 the
typical fishing ship averaged in size from 30
to 50 tons, but by 1620 Richard Whitbourne
was arguing that the ideal size was 100 tons[15].
Nevertheless there are reports of ships as
small as 10 tons making the transatlantic
crossing to engage in the fishery as well as
reports of others in the several hundred ton
category[16]. The size of the ship actually
varied depending on the scale of operations
employed by the financiers at home as well
the type of activity pursued in the
Newfoundland trade. In the beginning the

---

[14]Pope, 15.
[15]Cell, 3.
[16]Ibid, 104-12, 130.

fishery that emerged was that of a 'ship fishery' which meant that it was a purely migratory operation. West Country ships would arrive in their harbour of destination and pursue the fishery with their ship as base of operations. They constructed on shore only those installations necessary for their summer efforts and as soon as they dried enough fish to constitute a cargo the ship and all its crew sailed for home again.

By the 1590's the fishing ships were joined by a new type of vessel called the Sack ships[17]. Those were ships that did not engage in fishing but sailed the coast in search of cargos to purchase. They were all Dutch at first because there was a dearth of English shipping. London soon become involved and popularized this type of operation for their countrymen. Throughout the 17th century the navigation laws had their desired effect of driving the foreigners from the English carrying trade and thus the English merchants took control of the sack trade to Newfoundland as well.

Matthews reports that every aspect of the fishery in the 17th century lost money and many West Country merchants dropped out entirely[18]. Many events combined to inflict those setbacks. France had become self-sufficient in fish, denying the English a lucrative market. Then there was the competition from New England combined with bad weather and bad fisheries. Perhaps worst of all were the many wars of this century. James I (1603-25) inherited the Elizabethan wars against Spain and then in 1639-40 England was racked by the first and second Bishops Wars. The Civil Wars and the wars with Ireland occupied the whole period from

[17]Cell, 6; see also Pope, Chapter 3.
[18]Matthews, "West of England…" Chapter 5.

1641- 52. The conclusion of the civil wars
was followed by war with the Dutch for 1652-4
and war with Spain in 1655-59. The mid-1660's
witnessed war with Holland which was repeated
in the 1670's. As well, England was
continually at war with the Barbary Coast of
North Africa from 1664-89, the conclusion of
which was immediately followed by the
Jacobite Rising, the Irish War and the War of
the Grand Alliance to 1697. We must also
remember that the infamous Thirty Years War,
involving almost every state on the continent,
raged throughout Europe from 1618 to 1648.
Against this backdrop of disasters in the 17th
century there emerged the bye-boat fishery.

The insecurity which besieged the
fishery in the 17th century induced a shortage
of men and capital, poor markets and
uncertain catches. Entrepreneurial men of
the West Country responded by establishing a
bye-boat fishery carried on by bye-boat men.
These were fishermen who traveled out to
Newfoundland as passengers either on fishing
or sack ships and carried on a fishery in
Newfoundland by means of an inshore vessel
maintained in Newfoundland. They therefore
escaped the burden of building and repairing
transatlantic vessels and as their capital
outlay was very small they operated more
economically than the fishing ships. Bye-boat
men purchased their gear in England and
therefore accessed a cheaper market than the
resident planter. Many of the ship fishermen
initiated conflicts with the bye-boat keepers
as the latter were not only competitors for
fish and markets but posed a threat to the
fishing ship rooms in Newfoundland. They
continually pressed for restrictions on the
bye-boat keepers and while at times they were
partially successful eventually the ship
fishermen lost ground to the bye-boat keepers.
Matthews reports that by the 1680's the ship-

fishery had suffered so badly from the bye-boat keepers and others that it had almost disappeared and what remained was monopolized by the port of Dartmouth. By 1699 the English government recognized that the bye-boat keepers were there to stay[19].

But by-boat keepers and sack ships were not the only ones to keep company with the fishing ships on the coast of Newfoundland for a more threatening development had occurred on shore. Shortly after the great expansion of the fishery towards the end of the 16th century there occurred serious discussion about permanent settlement of the new possession[20]. As early as 1578 a Bristol man was arguing in favor of colonizing Newfoundland and the movement gained momentum in the following decades[21]. By 1610 another Bristol man, John Guy, had established the first colony at Cupids and his efforts were followed by those of several others in various parts of the Avalon Peninsula. Although those efforts failed as colonizing ventures many of the employees which they had brought out from England seem to have made permanent homes in various parts of the Avalon and became permanent settlers. Throughout the 17th century they were joined by hundreds of others who deserted the migratory fishery to begin operations as permanent planters. Those planters originated

---

[19]Handcock, W Gordon, **Soe longe as there comes noe women: Origins of English Settlement in Newfoundland** (St. John's: Breakwater Books, 1989), 27.

[20]For the best studies of settlement to date see Handcock; also John J Mannion, ed., **The Peopling of Newfoundland: Essays in Historical Geography** (St. John's: Memorial University of Newfoundland 1977); see also Head, **Eighteenth Century**; Pope, **Fish into Wine** and Keith Matthews, **Lectures on the history of Newfoundland, 1500-1830** (St. John's" Breakwater Books, 1988).

[21]For a discussion of those colonizing ventures see Cell, Chapters III-V

as the more entrepreneurial of the migratory
fishermen who saw advantages to remaining in
Newfoundland; they could secure their shore
installations from damage by vagrants,
aboriginal tribes, other fishermen or the
ravages of the weather. In addition they
could begin fishing earlier each year. By
staying year round they could also insure
they remained in possession of their
preferred fishing room as deserting it each
fall meant leaving it prone to be taken by
the first to arrive back in the spring. For
those and other reasons year round settlement
began in the 17th century and grew to such
proportions in the 18th century that settlers
came to dominate the production of fish. The
migratory fishery that once monopolized the
great codfishery was relegated to a minor
position by the 1790's and disappeared
altogether in the following fifty years.

In the meantime the old West Country
fishery had, for three-hundred years,
conferred immense benefits on the English,
and later the British economy[22]. Throughout
every age in England after the time of Cabot
one can find numerous references in the
literature of writers, merchants and
politicians holding forth on the great
benefits of the West Country fisheries. They
range from Prowse's claim that Newfoundland
was a virtual El-Dorado[23] to the statement of
an English politician in 1704 that the
fishery "was a more inexhaustible and
infinitely more valuable source of wealth
than all the mines in the world"[24]. Although
the truth about their real worth ranged
somewhere in between those grandiose claims
there is no doubt the Newfoundland fisheries

---

[22]Matthews, **Lectures,** Chapter. IV.
[23]Above, 21.
[24]Matthews, **Lectures**, 23.

were of quite substantial value to the
English economy. First of all, the fishery
provided employment for thousands of
fishermen and seamen each year. At its peak
as many as nineteen thousand to thirty
thousand men left the West Country each year
for the shores of Newfoundland[25]. As those men
and their ships required a huge quantity of
food, clothing, ship's stores and fishing
gear this fishery was a substantial market
for the agricultural and industrial
hinterland of the ports engaged in the trade.
The product resulting from this trade, the
very edible cod formed an important part of
the diet of the people of Europe and at the
same time its export by English merchants
earned much valuable foreign exchange for the
coffers of England. As the fishery also
employed hundreds of ships it fulfilled
perhaps its most important function for
English and British power politics, viz: it
trained the mariners and provided the naval
skills which were absolutely essential to
Britain's defense. Thus the West Country and
its fisheries played a significant role in
the social, economic, political and foreign
affairs of England and later, Britain, for
three centuries.

In addition to the benefits conferred
at home by the West Countrymen's pursuit of
the Newfoundland cod, they carried the flag
and helped found an international empire.
Today the great majority of the people of
Newfoundland and Labrador can trace their
origins to the West Country, primarily to the
counties of Devonshire, Dorset, Somerset and
Hampshire. Prowse gave pride of place to
Devon by maintaining that in the whole
history of England "there are no events more
remarkable than the doughty deeds of these

---

[25]Ibid, "West of England...", 409.

Devon men, who for a hundred and fifty years kept this colony for England and ruled over the thousands of foreign fishermen who resorted to the island"[26]. That is perhaps a more than slight exaggeration, as befits a son of Devon[27]. Nevertheless Gordon Handcock has shown that the largest block of Newfoundland's English migrants came from County Devon[28]. It is therefore no surprise to learn that Devon men played such a large part in the political and economic history of Newfoundland. Sir William Whiteway, Premier of Newfoundland from 1878-85, 1889-94, 1895-97, was a Devon man having been born in Totnes in 1828; another Devon man, A F Goodridge, who succeeded Whiteway in 1894, was born in Paignton in 1839. Two other Premiers had strong Devon connections for Hugh Hoyles, Premier, 1861-5, was the son of Newman Hoyles of Dartmouth while Sir Robert Bond, Premier 1900-08, was the son of John Bond of Kingskerswell. Other Devon men sat as members of the House of Assembly and at times were represented in both the Legislative and Executive Council. But it was in business that the Devon men in Newfoundland appear to have excelled.

Some of the most distinguished firms of Newfoundland originated in County Devon. Thomas H. Brooking, one of the principals in the old St. John's firm of Robinson and Brooking, was a Devon man. Benjamin Bowring, who founded the famous Bowring Brothers firm, belonged to Devon's capital city of Exeter. The Bulleys, of Bulley, Job and Cross, originated in Abbotskerswell. The Codners of Daniel Codner and Company as well as those of

---

[26]Prowse, 83.
[27]Prowse's father, the merchant, Robert Prowse, belonged to Torquay, Devon.
[28]Handcock, 146-7.

Codner, Alsop and company were all born in
Kingskerswell. The Duders of the firms Edwin
Duder & Sons, and Muir and Duder who operated
throughout the islands of Notre Dame Bay in
the 19th century, all came from St Marychurch.
The Goodridges who founded the family firm of
Alan Goodridge & Sons at Renews in the early
19th century were Paignton men. The famous
late 17th and early 18th century sea-faring and
merchant Holdsworth family of St. John's
called Dartmouth home. Newman Hoyles, one the
two principals in the founding of Brown,
Hoyles & Co in 1813 was also a Dartmouth man.
John Job who founded the well-known firm of
Job Brothers & Co hailed from Haccombe in
Devon. The principals in the firm of William
and Henry Thomas were natives of Dartmouth.
The famous Newman family, who operated in the
Newfoundland fisheries in some capacity since
the beginning of the 17th century and founded
the famous family firm bearing their name
which served the South coast until 1906,
lived in Dartmouth. Andrew Pinson, one of
the partners in the firm of Noble & Pinson
who operated in the Labrador fishery in the
18th century, came from Abbotskerswell. The
Rendell brothers, who founded the St. John's
firm of W & G Rendell, both belonged to
Ringmore in Devon. At least two of the
principals in the firm of Stabb, Row and
Holmwood, Row and Stabb, were born in Torquay.
While this is but a partial list it is the
firms in which the Henleys of Newton Abbot
were involved which concerns us here, and to
them we will now turn.

Chapter Two.

Henleys in the Avalon Fisheries

The earliest Henley connection with Newfoundland appears to have been in 1708 when it was recorded that Samuel Henley was a planter at the Isle of Spears on the Southern Shore[1]. We know from our knowledge of the Newfoundland fisheries that one does not become a planter without some previous experience on the trans-Atlantic fishing or sack ships, either as a crewman/servant or as a captain aboard same. It is quite likely that Samuel had been visiting the Isle of Spears for many years before he engaged in the fish business as a planter. In the following year, 1709, his name re-appears in the same area[2] and four years later he signed his name as "Samuel Hendly" in a petition to the Secretary of State[3]. The petition came from "...the inhabitants and merchants in Newfoundland ...." thanking the British government for the restoration of peace. Samuel was one of only one hundred people who signed the petition which from the context included those who were trading in and about the area of St. John's. As this list constituted a very exclusive club, it must be concluded that Samuel at that time was one of the principal inhabitants in the colony. In subsequent petitions to the British government over the next quarter century on which the planters, merchants and traders signed their names, there is no record of Samuel.

---

[1]St. John's, Memorial University, Maritime History Archives, Matthews Name Files, "Samuel Henley".
[2]Ibid.
[3]PANL, C O 194/14, f.53, c. 1713.

The paucity of records, however, renders it impossible to know more about Samuel's origins. We do not know whether or not he was a Devon Henley and the parish records of the pre-1700 period for that county are blank with regards to a birth of Samuel. The first Samuel on record in Devon was 1712 when a Samuel was born to William and Ann. But Samuel is a common name in later years amongst the Devon Henleys and we cannot rule out the possibility that Samuel of the Isle of Spears belongs to the same Henley family as that of Carbonear and St. John's. And the silence in the records following 1713 leaves us pondering a mystery. Whether he died or pulled up stakes for home still remains an unresolved puzzle. It is also possible that he ceased to be a planter and descended into the ranks of the servants, fated to be unlisted in the various records thereafter.

Because it was recorded that Samuel had three children in 1708 it becomes even more of a mystery that the name of at least one of them did not appear in the records in succeeding years unless they were all daughters. Unfortunately the records relating to the fishery contain few if any female names and their subsequent marriages would have masked the Henley name. Thus, it is quite possible that Samuel's death brought an end to the Henley name on the Southern Shore in the early part of the 18th century. Samuel's disappearance from the Southern Shore however did not bring an end to Henley connections with Newfoundland, for beginning in the 1750's there was a flurry of Henley activity in the trade and fisheries of this colony.

The middle years of the eighteenth century constituted a golden age of British Trade and colonial trade was especially favored. Throughout the period of the 1720's to the 1740's the British government carried out a series of measures to increase the export of British goods and encourage the import of those she needed. Those measures took the form of lower tariffs and export bounties. At the same time encouragement was given to entrepreneurs to finance this trade as well as to engage in shipping and the carrying trades. The ports of the West Country underwent a great expansion and Newton Abbot was one of those harbours which benefited from the increase in business.

The Henleys of Newton Abbot were therefore provided with golden opportunities to engage in the trade with Newfoundland. For not only was Newton Abbot a seaport town but it had become the regular place in the county of Devon for engaging hired hands for service in the Newfoundland fisheries[4]. The Henleys not only took to the sea but quickly appeared as artisans, master mariners, bye-boat keepers, ship-owners, manufacturers, tradesmen and merchants. Thus the Henleys of Devon established themselves in business at St. John's during the 1750's and 1760's and later expanded to Conception Bay and the Southern Shore. By the mid 1770's they had become so well established in St. John's that several of them were regularly serving on the grand jury and by 1777 Samuel Henley had acquired sufficient status to become elected as the grand jury foreman.

Around 1750 the Devon Henleys had established themselves as permanent residents in St. John's[5] and the names of various Henley companies begin to appear in the records. The earliest seems to have been John Henley & Co

---

[4]Sharpe, Rev. Alexander, "Newfoundland And Devon", *Newfoundland Quarterly*, Christmas, 1926, p.25
[5]St John's, C of E Parish Records, Marriages, 15 Nov 1759.

whose firm was operating a fishing establishment in St. John's by 1768. By the 1790's it had flourished to the extent that the company had engaged George Burton as a full time clerk and manager to assist in the operation of the business. It seems to have been employed strictly in the catching and curing of fish. However, by the 1820's the firm had expanded into shipping and mercantile operations. By 1830 records show that this company owned a fleet of schooners including the **Elizabeth**, the **George**, the **Jane**, the **Rachel and Ellen**, the **Rob Roy** and the **Three Sisters**. The firm had also taken on the responsibilities of dealing in provisions. But following 1830 we have not been able to discover any more references to this firm. Whether John Henley died and/or went bankrupt still awaits discovery amongst the few existing records.

Around the same time as John Henley & Co. first appears in the records, two additional Henley firms appear. By the early 1770's the firm name of Samuel Henley appears as a merchant in St. John's and is soon joined by William Henley & Co. Samuel first appears as a ship owner in St. John's in 1771 and by 1777 has become one of the principal inhabitants in the capital. In that latter year he was selected as the grand jury foreman. A census of St. John's properties in 1794 confirms that status, for Samuel is shown as the owner of at least three properties on the waterfront. While he continued to be recognized as a merchant of Woolboro, his home base, his principal source of income seemed to be his fishing establishment in St. John's. Records show that he later expanded his operations to include dealing in supplies and provisions for the fishery and the island's inhabitants. At the same time he formed a partnership with

two other entrepreneurs, William Codner
Henley and Richard Codner, to establish a
mercantile business in Renews. In 1820 Samuel
dissolved his connection with the Renews
business and continued his St. John's
operations until his death there in 1831.

Following Samuel's withdrawal from the
business at Renews, that firm, known as
Codner and Henley, declared bankruptcy.
Richard Henley, one of the partners, had been
a partner with Samuel in the earlier years of
the century. Together they owned several
schooners and were trading to and from the
Mediterranean, England and Newfoundland.
Following their bankruptcy at Renews, Richard
formed a partnership with a draper, John
Jardine, and continued as a ship owner and
trader.

Some time in the 1770's William Henley
& Co began business in St. John's. In its
early years this firm operated in the
catching and curing of fish. By the mid-
1780's William had a full time agent in the
person of William Ryan. At the same time he
established some connection with John Henley
& Co for the latter's representative, George
Burton, was acting for William as well. By
1786 William has gained sufficiently in
status to become a member of the Grand Jury
which means he had become one of the
principal merchants in St. John's. That
apparently came about as a result of a
partnership with a fellow entrepreneur from
Newton Abbot named Farley, and the firm was
named Farley & Henley. By 1795 this firm had
become bankrupt in Devon but William
continued in the St. John's business under
the name of William Henley & Co. He operated
an extensive fishing room on the St. John's
waterfront permanently staffed by four
servants. In 1799, however, the company
became insolvent in St. John's too. William

must have been a resilient person for he appeared again as a St. John's merchant under his own name and had earned sufficient respectability by 1804 to become elected as the grand jury foreman. In that same year he was leasing eight acres of land in St. John's but, to date, we have not been able to determine the purpose for which he leased the land. By 1817-18 the firm had become insolvent in St. John's.

When Samuel died in St. John's in 1831 it appears that he carried with him the corporate name of Henley. Nevertheless, the firm name had not disappeared completely from the Avalon Peninsula. In Bay Roberts a Mr. C. Henley of London had been carrying on business under the firm name of C. Henley and in Harbour Grace and Carbonear Samuel's sons were still involved in the trade and fisheries of the Colony. The Bay Roberts firm disappeared sometime before 1857 leaving only Samuel's sons in the business field. Samuel had founded a Carbonear branch of his St. John's company around 1799-1800 and had taken up temporary residence there by 1801-2. But when his sons matured sufficiently to take charge Samuel and his wife moved back to St. John's. That move could have taken place around 1820. Following Samuel's death in 1831 his sons James J. and Philip continued in the trade but on a much smaller scale. While they continued as ship owners, fishers and sealers, it does not appear that they engaged in the supplying business at all. While the families of James J and Philip pursued other interests outside the fishery the name of Henley ceased to be connected to the fishing industry in Newfoundland thus breaking a century old connection. And while the Henleys abandoned the Island fisheries around the mid-19th century they remained connected to those on the Labrador for some time longer.

Chapter Three

The Labrador Fisheries.

The names Hunt and Henley appear frequently in the 19th century archival records of Newfoundland and Labrador. The name of Hunt is especially prominent in the Labrador fisheries beginning in the eighteenth century but becomes rivalled with that of Henley in the following century. The oral traditions relate a similar experience. Alec Henley of St. John's preserves a two-century old oral tradition that the Henleys of Devon founded Henley Harbour as their original base of operations on that shore and the same traditions are re-echoed on the Labrador coast itself.[1] The Stone family of Henley Harbour has preserved the tradition that their original Labrador ancestor settled there around 1817. Perhaps a good way to determine exactly when the Henleys came to Labrador would be to trace the very origins of Henley Harbour.

Traditionally it had been believed that Henley Harbour was settled on or about 1774[2] but that was based on the assumption that the British fishery at Labrador had not begun until 1765 or afterwards[3]. On 24 Feb 1769 Newfoundland Governor Hugh Palliser urged the British government to amend the fishing laws to include the Labrador coast as there were so many fishermen frequenting that region. He reminded the British that Labrador had come

---

[1]Stone, Paul, "Henley Harbour: Fading into Oblivion?" *Downhomer*, St. John's, Feb 2001, 84-7; MHA: Bugden, Lorraine, "Henley Harbour 1971", a community study for History 3121.
[2]Smallwood, Joseph R, ed, **Encyclopedia of Newfoundland and Labrador** , "Henley Harbour", pp.906-7.
[3]Matthews, "West of England...", 400-06.

under their jurisdiction following the 1763 treaty of peace concluding the Seven Year's War. He said that twenty-seven fishing ships had established there in the summer of 1768 and in his fishery report for 1769 said there were eight ships fishing in the Chateaux area. I entertained the suspicion that one of those eight belonged to Henley and his name should soon appear in the records. But in spite of the numerous references to the merchants and traders in and around Chateaux Bay there was no mention of Henley, although I scrutinized the reports of Palliser and his successor-governors right up to 1784. For example, there is a petition to Palliser from forty merchants, traders and adventurers in Newfoundland dated July 1, 1770 but there is no Henley name affixed. For the years following 1770 there are many such petitions with names attached, but no Henley. The first time that the name Hunt (a later partner of Henley) was found in those records is Oct 3, 1771 when Edward Hunt appeared on a jury list for St. John's. And the first listing of a Henley company in St. John's was 1768 when the firm name of John Henley & Company appears in the records. As mentioned above there are several Henley references in the records of the 1770's at St. John's but none appear connected to Labrador. Then on Oct 16, 1784 a petition to the Governor from the Chief magistrates and Principal Inhabitants of St. John's includes the following entry amongst the signatures: "William Ryan for William Henley". Thus, I had gone ten years beyond the accepted date of 1774 and had drawn largely a blank with respect to Henley history on the Labrador. I began to think that perhaps they had been there much earlier than believed and had abandoned it for expansion further afield. So I examined the sources of those who had been repeating that founding date of 1774.

My study of those sources revealed that their patrons had not been using original records but had been quoting other published sources, principally George Cartwright's Journal. Immediately I began a careful search of those journals for references to Henley. That search proved that those who had earlier used the journal had not given it the careful attention it deserves. For on 19 Aug 1770 I found the following entry: "At sunset we anchored in Pitt's Harbour; and I immediately went to Henley Island".[4] As Henley Island had already been named by that summer of 1770 it might be reasonable to conclude that Henley had been there no later than the summer of 1769. A study of Cartwright's Volume I reveals that he talks about Noble, Pinson, Darby, Coghlan, Slade etc. but never once mentioned Henley or Hunt. He frequently visited Henley Harbour to buy salt from Perkins and Coghlan and I was puzzled as to why he never met or mentioned Henley or any of his men. Having closely read over a hundred pages in Cartwright's volume II, I decided to revert to the Governors' reports for the period pre-dating 1769. My suspicion was that Henley had been there even earlier and perhaps had either sold out to some other firm or was acting as agent for some West of

---

[4]Cartwright, George, **A journal of transactions and events, during a residence of nearly sixteen years on the coast of Labrador** (Newark : Allin and Ridge, 1792); Cartwright, who had been born in England in 1739, followed a military career from his early teens but in the mid-1760's came to Newfoundland to serve with Governor Palliser. From 1770 onwards he was involved in the cod, salmon, and seal fisheries of Labrador as well as the trade in furs. He kept a journal of his daily activities on the southern Labrador coast for almost two decades commencing in 1770; see DCB, V.

England company and was thus operating under a different name.

The famous historian D. W. Prowse declared that the West of England fishery in Labrador did not get started until after the Peace of 1763. But on 29 Nov 1762 there is a letter in Palliser's records from the Merchants' Hall, Bristol to the Board of Trade, London recommending the erection of a fort in the Straits of Belle Isle for the protection of the fishery there. This document raises doubts about Prowse's contention for the English Labrador fishery obviously pre-dates 1762. The Merchants Hall explained that "the fish in late years have shifted to the north...". There followed a letter from the Exeter merchants trading to Newfoundland supporting the above. It was signed by thirteen men.

This was a very good lead as there were many references to the Labrador fishery. In addition those records contained copies of the journals of four Moravian missionaries on the Labrador coast from May to November 1765[5]. The missionaries were Hill, Drachart, Haven and Schloerer who made their report to the Board of Trade on 5 Dec 1765. Their journal entry for 10 July 1765 is as follows: "...two of us went on shore on Henley's Island...". That entry proves that the name had been given to that island no later than the summer of 1764. We have now pre-dated the Henley connection with Labrador ten years beyond what was generally believed to be the case as well as revising the accepted date of the English origins of the Labrador fishery. There is reason to believe it began even earlier. Palliser had written the Board of Trade on 30 Oct 1765 in which he says that the grants made by Governor Murray on the

---

[5]PANL, C O 194, 16, f. 225

Labrador coast were now clandestine. Murray had become Governor of Quebec (which included Labrador) in 1759 following the battle of the Plains of Abraham and had made grants of fishing privileges on the Labrador coast to fishery adventurers. We must not rule out the possibility that West Country men, amongst whom was Henley, may have originally fished those harbours as early as 1760, or even earlier. In fact merchants from the west of England made proposals as early as 1752 for the opening of a trade with, and making settlements on, the coast of Labrador [6]. We must not discount the possibility that both Henley Island and Henley Harbour had been named by the Henleys as far back as the 1750's.

At the very least we could probably say that Henley had established himself at the harbour which now bears his name by the summer of 1764. It appears that he had entered the fish business there as an agent for a west country firm whose name evolved over time into Hunt and Henley. In the beginning the firm had operated under the name of Noble & Pinson, later becoming Pinson & Hine, then Beard and Hunt and finally Hunt and Henley [7]. In the McGrath papers there is a copy of a petition from the above firm to the colonial office, dated 1817, in which they said that they had established the first

---

[6]PANL, McGrath Papers, Box 8, Folder 1: from CO 5/1; " report of the Lords of Trade upon petition of several merchants containing proposals for opening a new trade and making settlements upon the Coast of Labrador", July 23/1752; those papers are the records of Newfoundland's renowned journalist, P T McGrath, who researched the case for ownership of Labrador, finally settled in the famous legal case against Canada heard in the Privy Council of the United Kingdom in 1927.

[7]Ibid, Box 5, folder 2 "memo in reply to the Canadian case", p.76.

fishery at Labrador in the summer of 1764[8].
This fits squarely with what we have
established above relating to the founding
date of Henley Harbour. It might be
reasonable to conclude that in the spring or
early summer of 1764 Noble & Pinson sent an
agent named Henley to Chateaux Bay, Labrador,
who spied Henley Island, sailed into the
harbour which now bears his name and made the
decision to found it as his base of
operations. If that were the case, where does
he belong on the family tree and what was his
first name?

The obvious place to look for the full
name of a businessman is in the company's own
records. But none of the records of either of
those companies have survived and we are left
pursuing a trail with very little evidence.
The only leads we have are the oral
traditions relating to Henley Harbour and
Henley Island, and of course the persistent
presence of those geographic names on the
coast of Labrador. Nevertheless a real
breakthrough seems to have occurred with the
survival of a court record from 1767. It
records a disturbance at Forteaux on the
coast of Labrador in Dec 1766 and one of
those giving evidence was John Henley[9]. It
seems that we have established a direct
connection between John Henley and Labrador
in 1766, just two years after the apparent
founding of Henley Harbour. Without evidence
to the contrary it is perhaps reasonable to
conclude that it was John Henley who
inaugurated the British fishery at Henley
Island and Henley Harbour almost two and a
half centuries ago.

But "reasonable" proof should never be
sufficient in the study of history for if

[8]Ibid, Box 9, folder 5.
[9]St. John's, MHA: Matthews Name Files, "John Henley".

such were the case it would be no different from writing a novel. I, therefore, sought verification from any and all existing records. In 2006 it came as quite a surprise to learn from the chief archivist of the Devon Record Office in Exeter that no records whatsoever have survived belonging to any fishing or trading company in Devon. Interestingly, in the national archives at Ottawa, Canada, can be found account books and correspondence from firms that operated on the Labrador coast from Quebec, maritime Canada and New England in the late 18th and 19th centuries. Although they don't answer my specific questions relating to the Henleys and Henley harbour, they do provide valuable information relating to the fisheries and fur trade of Labrador.

The most prominent firm that operated in Labrador in the 19th century was the Hudson's Bay Company. Their records have not only survived but constitute an historian's dream, for they are as legible and well-kept as records made today. Those records are a veritable gold mine on the social and economic life of Labrador in the 19th and 20th centuries. Within the first two minutes of searching those documents I discovered a surprising piece of information. That particular record maker said that in 1742 the Hudson's Bay Company had established a fur-trading post on the Albany River in what is now north-western Ontario and named it Henley House. My attention instantly leaped to England where the name Henley had for some time been very prominent in English national life and which, throughout the 18th century at least, could be found at many levels of politics and government. [10] The possibility that Henley Harbour had been named to honour

---

[10]Below, 92-3.

any of those well-known figures became quite a plausible option and may have had nothing whatever to do with the Henleys of Devon. But, one might ask, what about the John Henley who was there in 1766? Well he may simply have been a servant who worked for the usual 'one-winter-two-summers' term, then returned home and was never heard from again. As an example I refer to a record which I discovered at the Devon Record Office in Exeter. In 1757, a John Henley complained to the Overseers of the poor in Chudleigh that some of his masters had not been paying his wages.[11] In detailing his history he stated that he had been born in Wolboro, had worked for various masters over the years, and "after he was twenty-one went to Newfoundland...". Following his return to England his work history included jobs at various locations for six months at a time. Likewise, the John Henley found on the Labrador coast might have been just such a person. A careful scrutiny of all documents pertaining to Labrador show that never again does his name appear in any of the records.

Most important of all, the real significance of discovering Henley House was that it demonstrated the drawback of this particular method of constructing economic history. I had been pursuing a genealogical path in attempting to draw an economic profile of the southern Labrador coast, a path that is suitable only to constructing family trees. The wisdom of the genealogical approach is that you can proceed from the known to the unknown and in genealogy that is the safer route. But for economic, social or political developments this process is not suitable. For those kinds of developments the more reliable route is to choose a starting

---

[11]Exeter, DRO: Apprenticeship Indentures, P O 12/393.

point and by careful use of observable evidence to trace them forwards. As our quest lies in search of West Country roots in Labrador we will start with the first European contacts and move forward through the records carefully analyzing each and every "footprint".

The first Europeans to make contact with the coast of Labrador may have been the Norse who made occasional explorations there in the 10th and 11th centuries. They eventually made a settlement at L'Anse Aux meadows on Newfoundland island which lasted for a few years towards the end of the 10[th and] beginning of the 11th centuries. That settlement was permanently abandoned after a few years and neither at Labrador nor at Newfoundland did the Norse leave any permanent impact. We have hardly any evidence of further European contact with Labrador until well into the 15th century when Spanish fishermen arrived to fish the southern Labrador coast for the mighty whale.

At the Utrecht Peace discussions in 1713 Spain argued with England and France for a right to a fishery on the coast of Newfoundland[12]. Their negotiators claimed that Spanish fishermen had fished at Newfoundland as early as the 15th century. Although they lost the arguments their basic claims have recently been substantiated.[13]

---

[12]Matthews, **Lectures**, 104.

[13]On early European fishing in Newfoundland/Labrador waters see the following: Darlene Abreu-Ferreira, "Portugal's Codfishery In The 16th Century: Myths And Misconceptions" in Candow and Corbin, chapter Three; Barkham, Selma Huxley, **The Basque Coast of Newfoundland** (The Great Northern Peninsula Development Corporation, 1989); Ibid, **Guipuzcoan Shipping in 1571 with particular reference to the decline of the transatlantic fishing industry** (Reno: Desert Research Institute, 1977); Pope, Peter E, "The 16th century Fishery" in Candow and Corbin, Chapter Two.

The French soon followed the Spanish to the Labrador coast and Innis has concluded that by the time of Jacques Cartier's discoveries in the early 1530's Breton fishermen had already explored and named many of the present day harbours on the Labrador coast within the straits of Belle Isle. The explorations of the North American continent undertaken by the Canadiens following the founding of Quebec in 1608 are very well known. The average high school student can easily envisage the coureur-de-bois as they set out westward on their incredible adventures. However, what is not so well known are the explorations to the eastward. For just as the westward discoveries got underway so did French entrepreneurs commence explorations of the Gulf of St Lawrence and straits of Belle Isle. [14] By 1662 Quebec merchants had established fur and fishing posts as far north as Mecatina near the Belle Isle Straits and by 1715 had established fisheries at what is today known as St Modeste. By 1739 they had explored as far north as Esquimaux Bay and established posts involved in the seal, cod and walrus fisheries as well as in the fur trade. At the time of the British conquest in 1759 they had been happily fishing, hunting and trading in Chateaux Bay for more than twenty years. On the 4th of August 1760 Lieut James Webb sailed into their harbour on the HMS Antelope bringing bad news: the properties they occupied no longer belonged to the King of France but were now the rightful conquests of his most Britannic majesty, the King of Great

---

[14]On French and Canadien exploration of Labrador see Ottawa, LAC, RG 13, B4, Department of Justice, : "Labrador Boundary Case", vols. 7, 842; also Gosling, W. G, **Labrador: Its Discovery, Exploration And Development** (London: Alston Rivers, Ltd, 1910), Chapters III, IX.

Britain.[15] There followed a flurry of activity as Labrador licenses were granted to British merchants from Montreal and Quebec, who were soon joined by their brother-merchants on the other side of the Atlantic Ocean. Merchants and fishermen from Newfoundland soon followed.

Labrador unfortunately has received scant attention from historians. While a 'Labrador fishery' search at the Centre for Newfoundland Studies, Memorial University will yield approximately one thousand titles one would still be hard pressed to discover any comprehensive treatment of that particular subject.[16] Of those titles as many as 99% consist of journals, diaries, reports and surveys by various federal and provincial Fisheries departments, local and regional committee reports, bills, acts, political speeches as well as numerous briefs and representations to a variety of commissions and government bodies. Published monographic histories are virtually non-existent and the closest rivals are the few excellent productions by several sociologists and anthropologists.[17] For published works on the history of the Labrador fisheries one has to rely almost solely on the periodical literature. Fortunately several scholarly

---

[15]Ottawa, LAC, C O 323/15, 68: Webb to the Board of Trade 3 Feb 1761.

[16]For a comprehensive review of Newfoundland and Labrador historiography down to 2007 see Olaf Jansen at http://www.swgc.mun.ca/nfld_history/index.html

[17]Kennedy, John, **People of the Bays and Headlands: anthropological history and the fate of communities in the unknown Labrador** (Toronto: University of Toronto Press, 1995); Zimmerly, David, **Cain's Land Revisited: Cultural Change in Central Labrador, 1775-1972** (St. John's: Institute of Social and Economic Research, Memorial University, 1975); for a traditional account see Gosling, William Gilbert, **Labrador: its discovery, exploration, and development** (London: A. Rivers, 1910).

articles in that genre have been produced,
the principal ones being the writings of
Rothney[18] and Whiteley[19].

The neglect of Labrador is well
reflected in the character of the productions
by the History Department at Memorial
University. Since its inception that
department has generated one hundred and
thirteen theses in the Masters and Ph D
categories and forty-two Research Reports.[20]
But, unfortunately, not one of them concerned
the Labrador fisheries. In actual fact only
three of those writings focused exclusively
on a Labrador topic.[21] That same department
has generated two hundred and twenty one
Honors Dissertations but neither one of them

---

[18]Rothney, Gordon O, "The Case Of Bayne And Brymer: An Incident In The Early History Of Labrador" in *Canadian Historical Review*, XV, 1934, pp. 264-75.

[19]Whiteley, William H, "The Establishment of the Moravian Mission in Labrador and British Policy, 1763-83": in *Canadian Historical Review*, v. XLV, no.1, March 1964, pp. 29-50; Ibid, "The Moravian Missionaries and the Labrador Eskimos in the eighteenth century" in *Church History* 35 (1), March 1966; Ibid, "James Cook, Hugh Palliser, and the Newfoundland Fisheries" (St. John's: Newfoundland Historical Society, 1969; Ibid, "Newfoundland, Quebec and the Labrador merchants, 1783-1809 (St. John's: Newfoundland Historical Society, 1976); Ibid, "Newfoundland, Quebec and the Administration of the Coast of Labrador, 1774-1783" in *Acadiensis* VI: 1(Autumn 1976), 92-112; see also W A Black, "The Labrador Floater Codfishery" in *Association of American Geographers Annals*, vol. 50, 3, 1960, pp.267-95.

[20]The Research Report replaced the Master's Thesis in 2002.

[21]Bishop, John E, "Comment dit-on tchistchimanisi8 en français? : the translation of Montagnais ecological knowledge in Antoine Silvy's Dictionnaire montagnais-français (ca. 1678-1684) (St. John's: Memorial University, Research Report, 2006); Goudie, Nina, "Down North on the Labrador circuit : the Court of Civil Jurisdiction, 1826 to 1833" (St. John's: Law Foundation of Newfoundland and Labrador, 2005; Hiller, James, "The foundation and the early years of the Moravian mission in Labrador, 1752-1805 (St. John's: Memorial University, M A Thesis, 1967).

was devoted to any aspect of the fisheries of Labrador. Our myopic attitude towards Labrador pervades our entire literature on the province as a whole. One can search the numerous secondary works on this province and while copious Labrador references can be discovered each such reference generally constitutes but an appendage or afterthought to the main task in question. It is safe to say that Newfoundland's attitude to Labrador is best reflected by the provincial maps that used to be produced by the government in St. John's. On those typical maps you will discover that Newfoundland Island dominates the page while Labrador, approximately three times larger, is confined to a small inset in the top left hand corner.

The students of Labrador history, therefore, must depend largely on primary sources. Those records, fortunately, contain numerous references to that shore. They reveal that by the 1760's the southern Labrador coast, especially that part within the Straits of Belle Isle, was being mined for its cod, seal and salmon by a variety of West Country firms[22]. Those who resorted to Henley Harbour[23] found it a convenient and advantageous location for a cod fishery. Eventually the attractions of their secure base of operations enticed some of their transatlantic servants to enter the fishery on their own account. They soon became

---

[22]Ottawa, LAC, Earl of Dartmouth Fonds, vol 2, p.2394, Viscount Clare to Earl of Dartmouth, 18 Feb. 1773; also ibid, p.2434, George Cartwright to Dartmouth, 4 Mar 1774; ibid, pp.2438-45, Cartwright to Dartmouth, 12 Sept 1774; ibid, pp.2453-4, Cartwright to Dartmouth, 12 Dec 1774; P T McGrath, "Memo in Reply to the Canadian Case", McGrath Papers, Box 5, Folder 2.

[23]That harbour could well have been named for Robert Henley, b c.1708, the first earl of Northington, who became Attorney General in 1754 and Lord Chancellor in 1761.

settlers of Henley Harbour. One of the earliest of those settlers is believed to have been Charlie Stone, a native of Devon, who deserted his master's ship to begin fishing as an independent planter around 1817. Others followed and they were joined by fishermen from Newfoundland. By 1856 Henley Harbour had a population of forty three people. It remained a small community in terms of the number of people, yet it loomed much larger on the scale of business operations. Its attractions as a secure harbour close to a prolific fishery led to numerous transatlantic and Newfoundland firms following in the wake of merchants like the Nobles and Pinsons. In 1854, for example, there were fifteen independent business establishments operating in that harbour[24]. By that date the Henleys had long deserted the harbour that bore their name for greener pastures further north. In order to discover what had driven them from their original base we shall have to pick up the trail at the beginning of their adventure on the southern Labrador coast.

---

[24]Newfoundland, House of Assembly, Journal, 1854, appendix, 80.

Chapter Four

The Henleys in Labrador.

The Dartmouth firm of Noble & Pinson
was the first to establish a cod fishery on
the Labrador coast outside the Straits of
Belle Isle. They had been fishing at Conche
on the Northern Peninsula but news of more
plentiful fish north of the Straits led them
to establish a cod fishery in Chateaux Bay in
the late 1760's. [1] Shortly afterwards they
established sealing posts at Seal Islands,
Bad Bay and an additional cod fishery at
Temple Bay. In the period 1770-74 they
established salmon fisheries at St. Modeste,
Green Bay, St Peter's River, Niger River,
Mary's Harbour, and Hoop-Pole Cove, as well
as additional sealing posts at Seal Island,
Lance Cove, Antelope Tickle, and Fox Harbour.
The northward advance along the Labrador
coast was a continuous occurrence as
merchants like the Nobles, Pinsons, Hunts and
others sought out virgin territories free
from competition where they could start
afresh and steal a march on their competitors.
Making business profitable was becoming
increasingly difficult and every seized
opportunity had to be seen as an advantage
over your competitor.
The fishing industry had become quite a
precarious business for a variety of reasons.
First there were the difficulties attendant
on operating a fishery so far from home base
and being required to bring all supplies on
that far distant journey. Even after settled
establishments were made, virtually
everything had to be imported from Europe.

---

[1]Ottawa, LAC, Dartmouth Fonds, vol. 2, 2438-45, Charles Harbour,
Labrador, George Cartwright to Dartmouth, 12 Sept 1774.

Some merchants experimented with purchasing their supplies from Quebec but found it more expensive than European goods and abandoned the practice. Then there were the vagaries of nature that sometimes delivered up a reduced supply of fish and animals but often interfered with the prosecution of the fishery. Drift ice and heavy seas were serious enough at times to inflict severe losses on those involved. Added to those difficulties were the competitions offered by settled fisherman on that coast, plus the rivalries with migratory fishermen, planters and merchants from Newfoundland Island, as well as others from Quebec, the Maritime Provinces and New England. Merchants seeking to enhance their profits normally diversified by adding seal and salmon fisheries to their cod enterprises and entering the fur trade as well. Arthur Hunt added an extra strategy to those alternatives. While operating a firm under his own name and owning land establishments in the cod, seal, salmon and fur trade, he became part owner of other firms trading to and from the Labrador coast. For example he became a principal in the firm of Noble & Hunt and by 1809[2] had partnered with Philip Beard to take over the existing interests of the firms that had been known by the names of Noble & Pinson, Noble, Pinson & Hine, and Pinson & Hine. Hunt also became a principal in the firm founded by his sons in the 1820's under the firm name of C & E Hunt. Edward Henley, Arthur's agent, also became a partner in that firm and it eventually became known as Hunt & Henley. As well, Arthur was a significant investor in the London firm of Noble and Hunt. He received the usual benefits from such diversification but

---

[2]St. John's, PANL: Holloway to C O, 25 Feb 1809 in McGrath papers, Box 9, folder 6.

perhaps one of the most beneficial would be the opportunity offered by such alliances to profit from both sides of a transaction. For example Noble & Hunt sold some of their Sandwich Bay posts to Beard & Co in 1816. Arthur Hunt was part of the sales team but as a principal in the firm of Beard & Co he stood to gain from the purchase as well. Fortunately his extended family background had admirably suited him for commercial pursuits in those competitive times.

Arthur Hunt had been born into a prominent Dartmouth family in 1768. His father was William Hunt, a surgeon and his mother was Mary Holdsworth of the famous mercantile Holdsworth family involved in the Newfoundland trade and fisheries. Arthur had an aunt married to Philip Beard who was the agent in Labrador for the Dartmouth firm of Pinson and Hine. Arthur's brother, Thomas Holdsworth Hunt, married the sister of Sir Robert William Newman and their son became a director of the Bank of England. Another brother of Arthur, William Cholwich Hunt, married Mary Brooking of the famous Dartmouth Brookings firm involved in the Newfoundland trade out of Dartmouth and St. John's. Connections like those helped Arthur advance quickly in the world of business and at the age of twenty-one we find him in Ferryland as the agent for the firm of Robert Holdsworth. He was soon equipping ships and trading in goods and supplies with other firms around the Avalon. He built on this base to invest as part owner in several ships which he soon parleyed into full ownership of his first schooner. Then he appeared in the records as owner of a second ship and by 1814 he was the sole owner of at least five trans-Atlantic schooners. As his relatives, the Beards, were very active on the Labrador coast Arthur transferred his sphere of operations

exclusively to that scene and with Philip
Beard formed a partnership in the fisheries
as Beard and Hunt. They became the successors
of the firm that had previously been known as
Pinson & Hine and before that as Noble &
Pinson.

By the time Arthur Hunt arrived on the
Labrador coast his relatives the Pinsons and
Hines had already blazed the trails for him.
They, and their predecessors, Noble and
Pinson, had been operating on the southern
coast of that peninsula since the 1760's ,
beginning first in Châteaux Bay at Henley
Harbour and gradually expanding northwards
along that coast as far as Sandwich Bay.
Their business had consisted of operating
establishments in cod, seal, salmon and
furring. Their first efforts, like all other
West Country men in that trade, were
concentrated in the cod fisheries. Like them
they brought out hired fishermen, called
servants, who caught and dried the fish from
newly-erected buildings on shore. When they
left for the international markets in October
they would leave a few men behind to
participate in the seal fisheries of late
fall and early spring, as well as the winter
fur trade. As soon as they learned the lay of
the land they engaged men to fish the salmon
rivers, thereby becoming directors of a wage-
earning, year-round work force. But the same
natural tendencies that affected the men
servants further south on Newfoundland Island
set in there too, viz: servants saw
advantages to becoming permanent settlers and
originating a planter fishery on their own
account. The migrating fishermen responded in
much the same way as they did further south:
they began to move northwards in search of a
pristine environment where there was still no
competition in the cod and seal fisheries.
Thus by 1772 Noble & Pinson had reached

Sandwich Bay. When Arthur Hunt arrived on that shore in the early 19th century he joined with Philip Beard and took over those establishments that had already been developed between Chateaux and Sandwich Bays.

Perhaps what is most indicative of Arthur Hunt's success in the Newfoundland and Labrador fish business was his increasing stature in the social and economic life of his home port of Dartmouth, Devon. The surviving land records for Stokefleming show that by 1782 the Hunts were very prominent landholders, and by 1804 Arthur was the largest landholder there with twelve estates (one more than Arthur Holdsworth). His other relatives, the Pinsons and Hines, also involved in the Labrador fisheries, were prominently displayed there too. In Blackawton, from 1780 onwards, the Hunts and their relatives, the Hines, Pinsons, Cholwichs, and Holdsworths were the largest landholders. By 1782 Arthur Holdsworth was leading the way with twenty-three estates. The Cholwich family wasn't far behind at twenty-two. In Dartmouth, where Holdsworth again was the largest landholder, Arthur figured prominently as an estate proprietor. There he owned at least four houses as well as a large flour mill.

Arthur's Hunts success in the economic life of Dartmouth was recognized in the town's politics. That city was governed by an elected, eight-member corporation and in the decades following 1785 it was dominated by three families, the Holdsworths, Brookings and Hunts. Arthur's brother, William Hunt, served three terms as mayor in the 1790's and in 1798 Arthur joined him on council, becoming mayor two years later. He remained on council continuously up to 1815. Then, in the mid-twenties, he returned for two terms and in the mid-thirties for two more. At the period of the Irish uprising and in the midst of the Revolutionary Wars with France in 1798 Arthur Hunt was appointed Lieutenant in the Dartmouth Volunteer Association and a few months later 2nd Lieutant in the Royal Irish Regiment of Artillery. He proceeded gradually through the ranks until, before he retired from the Labrador trade, he became a Lieutenant Colonel.

Meanwhile on the Labrador coast Hunt had conscripted his Dartmouth neighbours and relatives by marriage, the Henleys, in his trading and business concerns across the Atlantic Ocean. During the later Napoleonic period John Henley appears as captain of one of his schooners while another Dartmouth Henley, Edward, was working at Hunt's shore stations. Sometime before 1817 the latter Henley had become Arthur's agent on the southern Labrador coast. Edward Henley's reputation as an astute businessman, well versed in the various Labrador fisheries, would soon become known up and down the Labrador coast. Sometime in the 1820's Arthur Hunt left the Labrador field exclusively to Edward Henley and retired to his Dartmouth office where he concentrated on ordering supplies and marketing cod, seal, salmon and fur.

When Henley found himself in charge of the firm he began to expand. The scene of his first expansion appears to have been Dumpling Island where he founded a new fishery sometime prior to 1817. An essential characteristic of fishing organizations on the Labrador coast seems to have been "movement", both laterally and geographically for the state of the cod fishery mandated that standing still meant disaster. Consequently merchants like Henley moved into additional sectors such as seal, salmon and fur, plus some new ones not contemplated by

Arthur Hunt when he had presided on that shore. The fishery on the Labrador had originated due to a scarcity on the coasts of Newfoundland. [3] Of course there had been intense competition on the waters adjacent to Newfoundland Island from the early 16th century onwards. As well there was a feeling by the middle of the 18th century that the fish had shifted to the northwards. By the 1760's it was widely believed, too, that the French, who were fishing around the Northern peninsula, possessed the advantage [4]. The founding of a British fishery on the coast of Labrador was then devised partly as a means to engage in competition with the French. But the northward movement did not stop with the founding of British establishments on the southern part of Labrador. For a scarcity of fish within the first settled bays led to a retreat to the coast and afterwards a northward movement along that coast. Sometime before 1817 Edward Henley, then the agent for the Hunt firm, founded a branch establishment at Dumpling Island. That was followed by the founding of branches at St. Francis Hr., Chateaux, Paradise, Divers Island, Long Island, Grady, Round I, Esquimaux Bay and Cartwright. It was in the latter place, once having deserted the Straits area, that the headquarters of the firm were established. Most, if not all of those branches, seem to have been founded in the 1820's and 1830's.

What type of operation did Henley carry on at Henley Harbour? As Henley was an agent

---

[3]It is my conviction that one of the chief characteristics of the Newfoundland and Labrador cod fishery in the 18th and 19th centuries was the scarcity of fish, and that the subsistence fishery perhaps emerged out of the transatlantic migratory fishery as an accommodation to this problem. I will explore this theme further in a forthcoming work.
[4]St. John's, PANL: C O 194/15, f. 45, Merchant's Hall, Bristol to Mr. Pownall. 29 Nov 1762.

for a firm located in the West Country it can
be said that he did, perhaps, what he was
authorized to do. Unfortunately we are not
privy to any of the internal communications
of that company as there are no known
existing records. Therefore we must surmise
that he carried out operations similar to
others involved in the Newfoundland trade.
From the totality of the records using many
disparate sources we can gather that Henley
would leave Devon, perhaps in April, loaded
with a variety of supplies for the
prosecution of the fishery. He would have had
on board a large crew possessed of a variety
of skills and talents. Once having landed at
his Labrador stations carpenters would
construct or re-construct stages, flakes,
stores, bunkhouses, cookrooms etc, while
other crewmen were engaged in catching and
curing fish. Henley would also have a number
of officials readying his articles for trade
with the natives. Several of the latter would
have been engaged to hunt for furs during the
winter and have sealskins ready when Henley
returned the following spring. In addition he
would have laid up a store of provisions for
sale to others who were frequenting the coast
from neighboring Newfoundland, Canada or New
England. Over time some of his crewmen
deserted to become permanent planters in
Henley Harbour and neighboring settlements.
He would then have expanded his operations in
the supplying business by catering to those
new settlers and, in return, buying their
fish.

While we do not have the exact details
of the operational transformations of the
Henley agency, we do have a basic framework,
but with estimated timelines only. In the
early years of their Labrador fishery it
appears that the Henleys confined themselves
to the Chateaux Bay region where they built

up their premises at various stations along
the Straits section of the southern Labrador
coast. In 1841 Captain Milne of the British
navy performed an inspection of the fisheries
on the Labrador coast and attempted to
provide a description of the usual type of
operations carried on by firms such as those
represented by Henley. He said those
establishments consisted of one principal
house which "...is in general a store for the
sale of the various necessaries of life, and
implements of fishing etc, and for the
purpose of purchasing fish from any casual
fishermen who come there. The superintendents
of these establishments generally come to
their house every spring, bringing with them
a number of fishermen to prosecute the
fishery, all of whom reside in temporary huts
during the season, and when it is concluded
return to England, St. John's, or their
native place, until the season commences in
the following spring"[5]. By the time Milne
visited the Hunt establishments, Henley had
already begun the tinning of salmon at the
Dumpling Island premises. The salmon were
packed in tin cases and exported to England.
Milne described the operations as follows:
"The salmon are cured at the rivers, which
are 20 miles from Sandwich Bay, packed in tin
cases, sent down to Dumplin Island, and from
thence shipped to England direct. The people
who fish the rivers, cure and pack the fish
in tin cases, are brought out from England in
the Spring, and again return when the salmon
is over, which is the beginning or end of
August. There are a few Indians in the
vicinity, who have come from the Moravian
settlements to the northward; they assist in
the fisheries during the summer, and are

---

[5]St. John's, PANL: Newfoundland, House of Assembly, Journal, 1851,
Appendix, 50-1.

engaged in procuring furs during the autumn
and winter, and in the spring employed in the
seal fishery, and all in the establishment of
Messrs. Hunt, between the Black Islands and
Huntingdon, at Sandwich Bay". Sometime later
they added a factory at Sandwich Bay for
tinning salmon as well.

The records of those days always
referred to even the humblest of persons by
the term "Mr." Thus it is only with the
greatest of difficulty that one can determine
a given, Christian name. For example there
are numerous references to Mr. Noble, Mr.
Hunt, Mr. Goodridge, Mr. Dawe, and Mr. Henley
etc, and quite often it is not possible to
determine a person's first name. The first
time that the agent's Christian name appeared
in the records was in 1817 when a court case
revealed that Edward Henley was witness to a
murder at Dumpling Island [6]. In 1826 the
sessions court at Dumpling Island referred to
him as "...agent for the trade of Arthur Hunt"[7].
Edward's name appears again several times
throughout the next decade but after 1850
there is complete silence in the records
regarding the name Henley on the Labrador
coast. However, the name Henley begins to
show up regularly on all correspondence from
the headquarters of the firm in London. That
development is explained by the fact that
Henley had become a full partner in the
company with Hunt and retired from the
Labrador coast to administer the business
from their offices in London. The Hudson's
Bay Company estimated that this partnership
had occurred around 1850 but I would be
inclined to place it much closer to 1840. On
his way to his Labrador station on July 17,
1836 one of the Hudson's Bay Co. men recorded

[6]St. John's, PANL, McGrath Papers, folder 3, p.6.
[7]Ibid, Box 10, folder 3, p.10

the following in his journal: "… cast anchor
this morning at Dumpling Island, where Hunt's
establishment is. Their supplies have not yet
been received from Europe. However about 11
AM Mr. Henley, one of the partners of the
firm, arrived in a chartered schooner, his
own having been crushed by the ice on the
island of Newfoundland, all the property lost,
also 8 men"… [8].

It should be pointed out that this
firm operated only in Labrador and did not
establish any branches on Newfoundland Island.
In 1863 they maintained "That they carry on
their business in and from England; that they
are (two only, we believe excepted) entirely
unconnected with Newfoundland…".[9]

Although Hunt and Henley may have been
unconnected with Newfoundland Island they did
maintain a complex network of connections
with the other firms involved in the Labrador
trade. Records that have survived from other

---

[8]St. John's, PANL, McGrath Papers, file 97, Hudson Bay Company
Journals: "Extracts from Journal of Occurrences of the Post of
Esquimaux Bay-Hamilton Inlet".
[9]St. John's, PANL: House of Assembly, Journal, 1864, appendix, p.
651: Newcastle to Bannerman, 2 Nov 1863, Encl # 1, Hunt and Henley
to Sir F. Rogers, Colonial Office; the comment "two only, we believe
excepted" is a reservation which still puzzles me; however there is
further evidence from alternate sources to confirm that Hunt and
Henley possessed no property in St. John's. In a list of the business
interests of St. John's who had suffered losses in the fire of 1846(CO
194/126, ff.417-18, also vol. 127, ff. 375-88, 580-3) there is no
Henley/Hunt listing at all; also on 21 Oct 1846 Charles Hunt from the
London office wrote to the Colonial Secretary claiming compensation
for losses suffered during the late fire at St. John's; he explained that
those losses were 50 chests of tea stored in the warehouses of E & N
Stabb (see CO 194/126, ff399-400); in other words the Hunt firm
possessed no property in the capital; however, this raises the question:
who was selling the tea for that firm? They must have had an agent but
the records have not yet yielded a definitive answer to this question
unless Stabb were in fact their agents too.

businesses along the coast confirm that they were interdependent. Arthur Hunt, Joseph Bird, C & E Hunt, Hunt & Henley and the Hudson's Bay Company did a brisk business with each other. For example when the Hudson's Bay Company ran short of provisions they purchased them from Hunt & Henley, Bird etc, and vice versa. In 1837 Bird was hiring youngsters in Devon for Hunt and paid their expenses out to Labrador. The costs were later recovered from Arthur Hunt. In 1838 the latter marketed fish cargoes for Bird. In other years Hunt's schooners brought out provisions for Bird's Labrador stations. In the same year Henley freighted salmon and oil to Liverpool for the Hudson's Bay Company and marketed the same there. In 1841 when Henley ran short of winter supplies on the Labrador coast he received them from the Hudson's Bay Company. In 1844 the Henley station at Sandwich Bay supplied the Hudson's Bay Company at Rigolet and in the same year Henley carried Hudson's Bay Company oil to London. In 1845 the Hunts brought out salt from London for the Hudson's Bay Company and the latter firm shipped their furs by Henley in the same year. In 1849 the Henley post at Sandwich Bay supplied the Hudson's Bay Company with wine, flour and shoes. The same pattern of trade between those firms continued from 1847 through to 1851.

From the Hudson's Bay Company correspondence we learn that the salmon fishery was just as insecure as the cod fishery. All firms, except Henley, avoided hiring salmon fishermen as they found it quite difficult to get the kind of skilled men needed to produce the prized salmon. Competition in that market was so intense that only very high wages could secure the workers required. Consequently they purchased their salmon from the local planters on the coast. Henley, however, never followed that practice but built up a solid, profitable salmon fishery by developing a secure, skilled and reliable work force on good wages. His salmon was so highly regarded in the market that his competitors could not compete with him on those grounds. They felt that Henley's experience and knowledge of the trade gave him a superior advantage. As one Hudson's Bay Company manager said, Henley was "...a clever, active man of business...". As a result in contemplating their bottom line in 1841 he warned the head office in Montreal that Hunt & Henley "...are the only House likely to give us any trouble from their habits of business and their enterprise they are ever on the watch, & whenever they see an opening they lose no time in availing themselves of it....″[10]

In the meantime Hunt & Henley had found the trade a demanding endeavour and, besides the employ of a trained and experienced work force, had been meeting the competition in a variety of ways. Some of those had been diversification of investments and production, variegated shipping and marketing, inter-connections with other competitors to induce a dependent relationship, as well as wholesaling and retailing. But their most important device was to drive ever and ever northwards along the Labrador coast. That was a tactic designed to elude the competition posed by the subsistence fishermen, and the migratory planters and merchants from Newfoundland Island. The chief advantage of this ploy was to discover new, pristine fishing grounds where the fish were still abundant. By the 1840's Henley had reached as

---

[10] LAC, "Report on the Coast Trade of Labrador", c. 1841, Esquimaux Bay District, Outward Correspondence Book, 1838-43, HBC fonds, Im217.

far as Cartwright, several hundred miles of coastline north of where the Hunts had first begun seventy-five years earlier. For several years he had been contemplating another, more risky venture that would take him into uncharted and un-fished waters on the remote northern Labrador coast. But a new kind of businessman had appeared on the coast and had been closely observing Henley's activities. Unknown to Henley this man had been negotiating with his head office to checkmate this resourceful entrepreneur.

Donald Smith had started out as a mere clerk with the Hudson's Bay Company but was destined one day to become its governor and major shareholder.[11] Canadians would come to know him as a famous politician and financier responsible for completion of the Canadian Pacific Railway. In 1848 the HBC sent him to North West River and he thus spent the next twenty years on the Labrador coast honing the skills that one day would make him president of the Bank of Montreal. Smith was continually taken up with how to outmaneuver his competitors, such as Hunt & Henley, and turn the HBC posts to profitable accounts.[12] Pursuant to this task he established new posts on the near-vacant northern Labrador coast. In the 1850's he re-established Aillik and in the 1860's founded a fishery and a trading post at Davis Inlet. Although Hunt and Henley did move further north by establishing a station at Davis Inlet they were soon met with competition not only from the HBC but also merchants from Newfoundland, Nova Scotia and New England. The competition for the scarce resources proved too intense

---

[11]**The Canadian Encyclopedia**, "Donald Alexander Smith", 1708; see also Donna McDonald, **Lord Strathcona: A Biography of Donald Alexander Smith** (Toronto: Dundurn Press, 2002).
[12]McDonald, Donna, Chapters 3-5.

and Hunt & Henley began the process of retrenchment. In 1850 Edward Henley's partnership with Arthur's sons, Charles and Edward, was dissolved. Henley continued in partnership with Charles Hunt with headquarters in London until 1861 when they dissolved that firm as well. In 1866 they sold their establishment at Esquimaux Bay to the Hudson's Bay Company and in 1868 the fisheries inspector reported that they had abandoned the supplying business at Long Island and Grady. In 1872 John Rorke of Carbonear purchased their establishment at St Francis Hr [13] and when they sold their Sandwich Bay premises in 1873 to the Hudson's Bay Company [14] , it appears that their association with Labrador came to an end.

---

[13] PANL: McGrath Papers, folder 8, p.9.
[14] Ibid, p.10.

Chapter Five.

Making A Living In Devon.

Before 1538 no Churches in England were required to keep records of their baptisms, marriages and burials. In the same year parliament placed that duty on all parishes but it took decades before churches could conform. In the 16th century, and early years of the 17th, few names appear and only those with some recognizable status were recorded. Nevertheless, by 1573 the name Henley began to show up in the Devon records and it became a regular occurrence after 1600. Those Henleys seemed to have been important enough to warrant recording of their baptisms, weddings and funerals. Because they were not a titled family their recognition in the Church records was deference to their status as landholders, significant enough to deserve the label of farmer. In 1630 Richard was the owner of a house and garden in Wolborough[1]and in 1641 Luke signed his own name to the Protestation returns in Abbotskerswell, one of only six out of the sixty-six males who wrote their own names. It's more than likely that he could read as "In the schools children began by being taught to read, and were not ordinarily allowed to use the pen until their reading ability had been established".[2]

The typical routine of those early 17th century farming families has been described for us by Laslett. "The boys and the men would do the ploughing, hedging, carting and

[1]Stirling, Rev D. M, **A History of Newton Abbot and Newton Bushel** (Newton Abbot: 1830), 32-3.
[2]Laslett, Peter, The **World We Have Lost**, (London: Methuen and Company Limited, 1965), 208.

the heavy, skilled work of the harvest. The women and the girls would keep the house, prepare the meals, make the butter and the cheese, the bread and the beer, and would also look after the cattle and take the fruit to the market. At harvest-time, from June to October, every hand was occupied and every back was bent. These were the decisive months for the whole population in our damp northern climate, with its single harvest in a season and reliance on one or two standard crops"[3]

The Henleys then had an early start as landowners and throughout the 17th and early 18th centuries amassed a considerable amount of land. Before the days of enclosure, farming the land consisted of ploughing strips of land acquired from the open fields surrounding every village. As family needs grew, more and more of the open fields came under the plough. The more enterprising of those families would have the opportunity to subject even greater areas to tillage and thereby increase their profits and consequently their stature. Families also added to their property pool by intermarriage and the Henleys, who lived in Newton Abbot and Abbotskerswell, benefited substantially from this network.

The land records which have survived show that by the beginning of the 19th century the Henleys residing in the region between Newton Abbot on the north and Tormoham on the south were amongst the largest landowners in the area. By 1800 they appear in the records as owners of at least twenty-four estates. Henley's Sherrill in Tormoham, was one of the largest estates in that town where a total of five hundred estates were found. They had added to their quotas substantially through the good fortune of well connected marriages.

---

[3] Ibid, 13.

In 1676 Sir John Stowell of Bovey Tracey transferred some estates in Abbotskerswell to be held in trust for John Shere, yeoman.[4] Then, in 1693 John Shere's son, by now a clothier, had become wealthy enough to purchase another twelve acres with cottages in the same area. John Shere Jr. had only one offspring, a daughter Mary, who married John Codner thereby bringing all those lands into the Codner family. When their direct descendant, Mary Codner, married Richard Henley in 1783 all the lands that the Sheres and Codners had amassed since 1676 passed into the hands of the Henleys of Abbotskerswell. Some of those lands were described as follows: "...3 messuages, 4 gardens, 6 orchards, 20 acs. of meadow, 20 acs. of pasture, 5 acs. of wood, 5 acs. of furze and heath & ¼ of the Abbotskerswell manor with appurtenances..."[5] The Henleys had now become one of the three largest landholders in the Abbotskerswell-Newton Abbot region and thus were well positioned by the 1790's to develop an agricultural empire. That was all the more possible because Devon's natural gifts had for centuries made it possible for that county to gain fame for its farmed produce.[6]

---

[4]Exeter, DRO: Indentures, 312M/TH 509; it is not clear from the indentures what relation John Shere stands to Stowell but he must have been his one and only relative.

[5]Ibid, 509, 512.

[6]The reports on the climate, soils, agricultural developments and economic history of England appearing in this work are based on the following sources: Birnie, Arthur, **An Economic History of the British Isles** (London: Methuen & Co Ltd, 1969); Coppock, J. T., **An Agricultural Geography of Great Britain** (London: G Bell & Sons, 1971); Court, W. H. B, **A Concise Economic History of Britain From 1750 to Recent Times** (Cambridge: University Press, 1954); Deane, Phyllis and Cole, W A, **British Economic Growth 1688-1959** (Cambridge: University Press, 1964; Drummond J. C. and Wilbraham,

Devon's climate and soil are such to have made Devon and much of the West Country the most favorable places in England for agriculture. Its climate is famous for its mildness and even in January the mean temperature lies between forty-two and forty-four degrees Fahrenheit. But perhaps the numerous rivers are the greatest natural gift in Devon. Flowing from the great tableland of Dartmoor they bring life to the entire county. Especially in the south they enrich the sheltered valleys and the lowlands, helping to create the flowers and fruit orchards for which Devon has become famous throughout the centuries.

Devon was amply suited for an agricultural economy and that was not very different from England as a whole. For throughout history England had been an agricultural state, and even after the Industrial Revolution had begun agriculture remained by far the largest sector of the economy and continued to be so well into the 19th century. But in the second half of the eighteenth century an industrial revolution had begun to transform the English economy and its effects were felt on agriculture as well. In south Devon the Henleys had been

Anne, **The Englishman's Food: A History of Five Centuries of English Diet** (London: Pimlico, 1994); Havinden, M. A, **The South West And The Land** (Exeter: University of Exeter, 1969), Marshall, William, **The Review And Abstract Of The County Reports To The Board Of Agriculture, vol 5: Southern and Peninsular** (York: Thomas Wilson & Sons, 1818); Ibid, **The Rural Economy Of The West Of England, vol I** (London: G Nicol, 1796); Mathias, Peter, **The First Industrial nation: An Economic History Of Britain, 1700-1914** (London: Methuen & Co Ltd, 1969); Murphy, Brian, **A History of the British Economy, 1086-1970** (London: Longman Group Limited, 1973); Vancouver, Charles, **General View of the Agriculture of the County of Devon** (Newton Abbot: David & Charles Limited, 1808).

farming the land nigh on two centuries while the famous orchards had served their individual needs in ways Devonians had been accustomed for centuries. They had been known to be daily drinking cider as far back as the Middle Ages and continued this tradition well into the seventeenth century, when other Englishmen were drinking ale or beer. In Devon cider still reigned supreme. Apparently everyone who held a piece of land made their own cider and it held such a prominent place in daily life that by 1794 it formed part of the daily wage to pay a worker one shilling plus a quart of cider.[7] But improved methods, new inventions and expanding markets propelled the Henleys to take cider production to new levels and soon transformed the fruits of those lands into a manufacturing empire. Thus in 1791, at Abbotskerswell, the Henleys founded a cider factory, the first of what would eventually become a national chain of cider factories throughout England.

After 1790 demand in the London market grew enormously for such rural products as meat, cheese and cider. That market continued to grow throughout the nineteenth century and the Henley factory at Abbotskerswell targeted that market from the beginning. Nevertheless they produced for the export market as well and many of the St. John's merchants regularly imported Devonshire cider and advertised its sale in the local papers.[8]

Some time in the 1830's the Henleys opened an office in London on Tooley Street. It appears that this was at first a

[7]Fraser, Robert, "General Review of the County of Devon, March 1794" in Marshall, **The Review...**, 551.
[8]See for example, *The Public Ledger*, St. John's, 28 Apr, 2 May, 7 June, 1837; 6 Jan 1843; *Royal Gazette*, , St. John's, 1 Aug 1837; *The Times*, , St. John's, 4 Feb 1852.

distribution office, but business soon proved so successful that they expanded. They had begun business in Devon as cider makers but now in London they added the manufacturing of ales and stout. By 1882 they had opened plants at Joiner Street for those purposes. At the same time they entered the business of importing and distributing wines and spirits. Then they established a new plant at Long Lane for the manufacture of vinegar and in the 1890's they added cordials[9] to their list of manufactured products and shortly after 1900 began the manufacture of wine. They also entered the international markets as exporters of their ales, stouts, vinegar, cordials, wines and cider. At the same time they entered the import business, bringing in American sweet cider for retail in the English market.

In the second half of the 19th century Henley & Son underwent an enormous expansion of their business in Devon. They expanded their operations at Abbotskerswell to include, in addition to their main steam mills, the building of new cellars. To those they added Main Stores at Abbotskerswell and then to celebrate the jubilee of Queen Victoria, in 1897, they built new stores which they named Jubilee Stores. During this same period they opened new offices and plants at Blagdon, two Stores at Pinhoe and began four operations at Paignton.

In the 1870's they established a new branch of the business in Kingsbridge, Devon. William Bond, a local merchant and insurance agent, was placed in charge of their office there. At about the same time they opened new offices and stores at Newton Abbot, and vinegar was added to their list of manufactured products. This expansion

---

[9]A cordial is a liqueur.

continued and by the 1890's they had established twenty-one plants in south Devon.

At the famous Paris international exposition in 1867 they displayed their products before an international audience and won prize medals for quality. According to the *Illustrated London News* their Perry "…was much admired by the jury…"[10] and consequently it was awarded a bronze medal. Their vinegar and cider also received bronze medals. They opened a display again at the international exposition in Amsterdam in 1869 and won a bronze medal. They also repeated that performance at the Lyons exposition in 1873. But their crowning glories were the prize medals they won at the international expositions at London in 1873 and in 1875.

Around 1895 they opened a new depot at Ledbury in County Hereford. That town was an advantageous location for a new depot and even by the time Henley and Sons arrived the town already had fourteen cider merchants. Ledbury was a union and market town, as well as being a parish, head of a county court district and polling place. It was only 120 miles from London by road, and the Worcester and Hereford section of the Great Western Railway passed through the town. It was the junction as well of the line to Gloucester. Cider and Perry were already manufactured there in large quantities for the whole county was famous for its rivers, soil and luxuriant vegetation. "…the country is clothed in almost perpetual verdure", said Slater in 1868, "on every side a luxuriance of vegetation is exhibited, in widely-extended corn fields, teeming orchards, expansive meadows and flourishing

---

[10]*Illustrated London News*, vol 51, Supplement, 14 Sept 1867, 308; perry was a fermented liquor made from pears.

plantations...".[11] It was already famous as a cider county and by the time of Charles I was well noted for its apple orchards. Two years after they arrived in Hereford the Henleys added another and more substantial property to the one they already possessed.

In the early 1890's they added an outlet in Bristol, a city and port already well known for its vinegar trades. The National Fruit and Cider Institute was associated with Bristol University for purposes of agricultural and horticultural research and advice. In that city the Henleys added the manufacture of cordials to their cider growing, refining and exporting. They also acted as wholesalers at Bristol and contracted two mercantile firms, A C Clark & Co Limited and William Henry Colcock, as their agents. However, sometime just prior to World War I they closed out their mercantile associations with the city of Bristol.

In 1904 Henley & Son purchased the business of the French Vintage Company of Devon who were the proprietors of "Sparkling Avalon", an exquisite champagne which the company continued to make "...from the apple in the same way that champagne is made from the grape".[12] The French Vintage Company had been established at Broadclyst in 1877 but William Codner Henley, the then company owner, moved the operations to Newton Abbot. There, Henley & Son continued the manufacture of champagne which they claimed would "... retain all its good qualities and remain bright and sparkling for years".

Following World War I the Henleys pursued a policy of consolidation for the

[11]**Slater's Directory of Gloucestershire, Herefordshire, Monmouthshire, Shropshire & Wales, 1868**: "Herefordshire", 1.
[12]Kew, TNA: Registrar of Joint stock Companies, "Prospectus", Henley & Son's Cyder Company Limited, 1921.

more effectual production of an extended product line. Heretofore they had operated as a family business under the name of Henley & Son but now they incorporated a new company under the style of Henley & Son's Cyder Company Limited. The new company acquired all the assets of the former family business as of October 1, 1920, while the owner/operator of the family concern, William Codner Henley of Ipplepen, Devon, became the Chairman and Consulting Director of the new company. His son, John Leaman Henley, became the managing director at Newton Abbot. William Codner Henley, who had first started in the business in 1884, retained control of the company by taking twenty-five thousand of the fifty-thousand cumulative preference shares issued as well as taking forty-three thousand, three hundred and forty-three of the sixty-five thousand ordinary shares.

By the time of incorporation in 1920 Henley's Cyder had become the best known and most highly regarded article of its class in the United Kingdom. In addition William Codner Henley, the owner, claimed that due to its exports his company's products had become "...extensively known and appreciated in various parts of the world". As a result the properties in land, plant and machinery etc of the family operation were valued at £100,000 at the minimum.[13]

Heretofore the company had, since 1791, specialized in the manufacture of cider but in forming the new company they pinned their hopes on champagne. Thus the new firm intended to increase the production of that drink. For that purpose additional capital was required and thus the new company was

---

[13]Small items like cases, casks and bottles etc were, for purposes of sale to the new company, valued at less than half their cost by Codner Henley.

formed. The expansion began first with the consolidation of existing operations. The firm had already been pursuing a consolidation since the turn of the century and during World War I they had contracted their operations in London, confining themselves to the one location near London Bridge. The new operation continued the consolidation by closing out stores in Devon at Pinhoe, Blagdon, Paignton, Ashburton and Totnes. By those closings they hoped to effect huge savings in transportation and storage. Those operations were then centralized in the towns of Newton Abbot and Abbotskerswell. The new capital created by the issuing of stock in the incorporated company was then applied to the purchase of new premises, acquisition of new machinery and construction of a new steam mill.

Following the introduction of the new organization the company began to stress the health and hygienic qualities of their products. The south Devon coast had become a prime tourist attraction and the Henleys opened their plant in Abbotskerswell to this new trade. Their guided tours placed an emphasis on healthy drinking and as a result of this new strategy the firm won the Gold Seal Certificate from the Institute of Hygiene in 1932. [14] But in spite of those modern tactics and the excellent quality of their products the firm suffered from the far-reaching economic down-turns taking place in Britain and throughout the world. In 1933 they went into voluntary liquidation and eventually sold out to a rival cider manufacturer, Whiteways of Whimple. The latter company continued to operate the

[14]Jones, Roger, **A Book of Newton Abbot** ((Bradford On Avon: Ex Libris Press, 1986), 46-7.

Abbotskerswell factory for another thirty years before being forced to close its doors for good in 1965.

The periods following both World Wars were very unkind to the British economy and the repercussions were keenly felt by the Henley cider business as well. The post World War I period witnessed serious setbacks in Britain's largest industries that once had led the world. They now faced serious competition from new and more modern economies such as the United States. At the same time the inter-war period was plagued by strikes, political crises and the economic depression of the 1930's. The older fruit orchards suffered heavily from increased competition in novel drinks but especially from new farms. The Devon fruit industry lost ground steadily to orchards in Essex, Norfolk and Sussex. Those problems were compounded in the aftermath of World War II. By the 1960's the British economy was buffeted with huge government deficits, heavy borrowing, unfavorable trade balances and escalating prices and wages. Perhaps the basic problem was that British industry which had once led the world had lost its competitive advantage earned from both an early start and a near monopolistic position. Thus the modernization of factories was the greatest challenge and government assistance and leadership were made available. This was no less true for agriculture and after 1960 old orchards were taken out of production and replaced with newer ones that tended to be closer to London. In addition the great majority of new orchards were planted with dessert apples and pears "… a crop some three times as valuable as cooking apples and seven times as valuable as cider apples…." [15] Thus the old orchards,

---

[15]Coppock, 293

especially those in the south-west, lost ground heavily to newer farms and more consumer-oriented products and drinks. Against that background the Henley Cider business closed out all their operations outside Devon and retreated to Abbotskerswell where they had first begun in 1791. In the mid-1930's they sold their remaining operations to a competitor and in the mid-nineteen-sixties the Abbotskerswell plant closed its doors for good. In 2007 it was turned into a Business Park housing a mixture of engineering and industrial firms.

Chapter Six.

Modern Manufacturing in St. John's.

When the first official government census of Newfoundland was taken in 1827 it revealed that near ninety-five percent of the people depended directly on the fishery. That was a simple way of life based on the catching and processing of salt cod that has become known as Newfoundland's traditional economy. In the half century following 1827 little changed in that field. However the half century following 1869[1] witnessed serious efforts to diversify Newfoundland's economy and add a manufacturing base to the traditional activities.

Following defeat of the Confederation proposal in the 1869 election, Newfoundland politics increasingly became an arena for debating economic alternatives to union with Canada. One politician summed up the options in a now famous sentence. There were only four choices facing Newfoundland, said E P Morris, Assembly member for St. John's West, and they were "...starvation, emigration, Confederation or opening up the country".[2] As few people could be found supporting Confederation following its defeat in 1869, politicians concentrated on the remaining

---

[1]1869 was a watershed year in Newfoundland's history for in a general election of that year Newfoundlanders rejected, by a wide margin, Confederation with Canada; for discussion and analysis see James Hiller, "Confederation Defeated: The Newfoundland Election of 1869" in Hiller, James and Neary, Peter, eds. **Newfoundland in the Nineteenth and Twentieth Centuries: essays in interpretation** (Toronto:, University of Toronto Press, 1980), 67-94.
[2]Newfoundland, House of Assembly, 14 May 1889.

list. [3] While starvation could never be a
deliberate choice and as emigration was
political suicide for a politician, debates
centered around ways and means of opening up
the interior of the colony. Circumstance
would prove there was no shortage of ideas in
this sphere as Newfoundlanders generated
every possible alternative. These ranged from
borrowing a likeness of the sophisticated and
now-famous national policy of John A
MacDonald in the sister Canadian colony, to
others much less credible and to some that
were downright ludicrous. Debate however
centered mainly around building railways to
access the interior where it was hoped
settlements would spring up to take advantage
of the mining, forest and agricultural
resources of which, it was presumed by all,
Newfoundland possessed a super-abundance.

Above all Newfoundland's political
leaders concentrated on drawing people away
from the non-productive fisheries towards a
manufacturing base to be established under
government leadership and patronage. At the
end of this period manufacturing remained,
relatively speaking, insignificant in terms
of the colonial economy yet there were some
impressive gains both quantitatively and

---

[3]For a good survey of the political and economic issues surrounding
development and under-development in Newfoundland see Summers,
Valerie A, **Regime Change In A Resource Economy: The Politics of
Underdevelopment in Newfoundland 1825-1993** (St. John's:
Memorial University, 1993), Chapters 1 and 2; also Alexander, David
"Newfoundland's Traditional Economy and Development to 1934" in
Hiller and Neary, 23-37; Hiller, J. K, "A History of Newfoundland,
1874-1901"(Cambridge: University of Cambridge, Ph. D Thesis, 1971);
O'Flaherty, Patrick, **Lost Country: The Rise and Fall of
Newfoundland 1843-1933** (St. John's: Long Beach Press, 2005), 111-
18, 221-3, 230-2, 250-2, 310-12, 331-2, 339-40.

qualitatively.[4] A plethora of little factories were established in this period, especially in St. John's. There, the newspapers were gushing almost every day with news of the opening of yet another factory. In that city the bakery and confectionery industry became the largest employer in the perishable goods sector, for by the mid-1870's six major factories were operating in that field. New manufacturing concerns were also opened in the clothing sector, in boots and shoes, ropes and twines, cooperage works, in iron and steel, and in furniture. Over all per capita output almost doubled in the 25-year period following 1884, rising from $7.28 in the former year to $11.61 in 1911.[5] And in the period between 1910 and 1939 per capita growth in Newfoundland was higher than it was in Canada.[6]

The procedures by which Newfoundland governments sought to encourage secondary manufacturing in the period 1870 to 1934 involved the combined efforts of special legislation and tariff protection.[7] The former took various forms such as subsidies, bounties, premiums, drawbacks, grants of money and/or land, free power and tax exemptions. The tariff was also manipulated to provide free imports of machinery that could not be made in Newfoundland, duty free raw materials and a reasonably protective

[4]Joy, John Lawrence, "The Growth And Development Of Trades And Manufacturing In St. John's 1870-1914" (St. John's: Memorial University, M A Thesis, 1977), 2-9; Alexander, David, "Economic Growth in the Atlantic Region, 1880-1940" in Sager, Eric W, Fischer, Lewis R and Pierson, Stewart O, compilers, **Atlantic Canada and Confederation: Essays in Canadian Political Economy** (Toronto: University of Toronto Press, 1983), 51-78.
[5]Ibid, 18.
[6]Alexander, "Economic Growth in the Atlantic Region", 69.
[7]For an excellent account of those efforts see Joy, 13-16.

tariff on manufactured goods made in the colony. Under this umbrella of government encouragement to industry the Henleys made their appearance once again in the business field in St. John's.

Following the death of Samuel Sr. in 1831 there followed a period when no Henley business operated in St. John's. James J. and Philip were still located in Carbonear but the Henley business connection with St. John's was re-established when James J's son, Charles, married there in 1869. Charles had begun his working life at sea aboard various steamers until he became purser on the Curlew. His many trips to the United States became an opportunity to learn about the fishing business between there and Newfoundland. He made a decision to establish some kind of fish business based in St. John's but with some connection to New England. On one of his visits to Boston he contracted pneumonia and was just on the verge of establishing a company when, in 1882, his career was cut short by a sudden, early death. His career was so brief as to deprive us of the information necessary to determine some details of his operations. Because his family members were all quite young, he had no logical successor and his business must have died with him. Thus, when Charles's son, John J., went out to work at age fifteen he apprenticed himself to a furniture manufacturer, Joseph Daymond in St. John's.

Daymond's factory was one of the many little factories that had been established in St. John's in the last quarter of the 19th century. It concentrated on the making of chairs, tables and bedsteads. There John J. Henley honed the skills of his trade and earned distinction as an expert craftsman in the upholstering field. Following his apprenticeship at Daymond's he left to become

an acknowledged master at Callahan and Glass,
an upholstering company. There he became
known as the man who designed the wooden
slides for the mattress box. He could most
likely have remained there his entire working
life becoming the premiere craftsman of his
time but John J. was a man of ambition and
possessed the entrepreneurial spirit of the
original Henleys. Consistent with the Henley
tradition John J. embarked on a new career in
1903 when he established, on Henry St in St.
John's, the much heralded mattress factory.
Thus he re-established the corporate name of
Henley which had first graced the pages of
Newfoundland business history almost 150
years previously.

The great difficulty in discussing the
mattress factory history is the fact that
none of the records of the firm have survived.
So we can not even be certain of the exact
date of its beginnings. However, we know he
operated under the firm name of John J.
Henley and took out his first newspaper
advertisement on Jan 30, 1904. [8] That would
point to 1903 as the establishment year. Also
the Evening Telegram in its obituary of John
J. Henley in 1942 said he had established his
factory in 1903. [9] We can thus settle on that
year as the founding date, with the
reservation that it is not derived from a
first hand source.

Normally, not knowing the exact year of
the founding of a company or factory would
not be considered especially significant but
in this case there are exceptional
circumstances surrounding the opening of
Henley's factory. For, although several
mattress factories would soon make their
appearance in St. John's, Henley's was the

---

[8] *The Trade Review*, St. John's, 30 Jan 1904.
[9] *The Evening Telegram,* St. John's, 16 Feb 1942, 3.

first such factory in the history of Newfoundland. A perception had been growing for some time that the old feather beds breathed disease and were not considered healthy. [10] Henley became the first to take advantage of this new cultural swing and was soon doing a booming business. Within a year or two of the opening of new mattress factories a craze had grown amongst the public for the new product. "It looks now", commented a St. John's journalist, "as if in a few years, we will have to go to the museum to find a feather bed". [11]

Henley billed himself as an upholsterer by trade and at 16 Henry Street in the capital, began the manufacture of mattresses, spring beds, cushions and parlor suites. He quickly acquired such a large share of the market that it became the talk of the town. Whether it was his reputation as a skilled tradesman or the unique popularity of the new product, he soon had more business than he could handle. [12] Less than two years after he had begun operations the *Trade Review* reported that he had large contracts with local dealers for the retailing of his products and "...he bids fair to build up a good trade". [13]

Henley also took advantage of his upholstering skills by adding as many kinds of upholstering as he could find in the local market. He apparently made a specialty of the upholstering on passenger steamers. In that area he made large demands for local materials such as marine grass. Locally termed, "goose grass", he offered $30.00 a ton to suppliers and soon it was being

---

[10]*Trade Review*, 27 May 1905.
[11]Ibid.
[12]Ibid, 30 Jan 1904.
[13]Ibid.

delivered from all across the island. Conception Bay, however, supplied most of his material in that field. His business was so good in those early years that he enlarged his factory by acquiring the building next door to the original factory on Henry Street. While mattress making remained the principal concern of the factory, by 1907 he had made a specialty as well of upholstering settees and chairs. Demand was reportedly so great for his products that he had, in that year, almost completely displaced the imported articles in that field.

He was continually finding new outlets for his products such as the sealing vessels and the lumber camps. And sometime in the pre-World War I period he diversified his production. To his previous product line he added the manufacture of couches, chairs, pillows and bolsters. Demand grew so fast that expectations arose that he would soon found a second plant. But World War I dampened his plans somewhat and his expansion plans were delayed. However by the nineteen twenties demand for his products had grown to such an extent that he fulfilled a long-standing plan to establish a second plant. He purchased land on Kenmount Road for that purpose but soon changed his mind and took a location at the corner of Newton Road and Empire Avenue. There he erected his second factory and in the mid-1930's introduced to this province the manufacture of the first mattress springs, locally named "The Starry Night". Simultaneously he began the production of Newfoundland's first box springs.

In 1917 R. G. Dun & Co of Calgary sent a business expert to St. John's as part of a Canada wide survey of businesses. He placed the pecuniary strength of J. J. Henley & Son at that time in the range of $3000 to $5000

and gave it a general credit rating of
"fair". [14] In 1922, however, the Bradstreet
Company of New York engaged in a similar
process. They placed the worth of the company
in the category of $5000 to $10,000 and
labeled Henley's credit rating as "first
grade". That perhaps is the best yardstick of
the company's progress and success in its
very brief operational history to date. In
1932 Bradstreet returned and in spite of the
Great Depression reassessed the company's
worth and placed it in the $10,000 to $20,000
range. At the same time he assigned it their
highest credit rating for firms in that value
range.

In 1928 Henley took part in a province-
wide slogan competition and came out in first
place. His winning slogan was "wide awake
when you buy them, sound asleep when you try
them". By the nineteen-thirties it was
reputed that he was supplying at least two-
thirds of the bedding in the Newfoundland
market. [15] At its peak the Henley business
employed upwards of twenty-five workers, to
all of whom he paid rates above the union
levels then prevailing in St. John's. When
union organizers approached his factory to
promote unionism John J. welcomed them and
encouraged his workers to join. But the
Second World War compounded the difficulties
of obtaining regular supplies of spring-
making material and early in the war period
he closed out the Newtown Road factory to
concentrate on the Henry Street plant.

John J. schooled several of his sons to
follow in his footsteps. He promoted Leo to
manager in the mid-1930's but then tragedy
struck as Leo was cut down by tuberculosis in

[14]**Mercantile Reference Book 1917 For The Dominion Of Canada**
(Calgary: R G Dun & Co, 1917), 343.
[15]Alec Henley, interview, 2006.

1936. A celebration of sorts took place in 1941 when John J. celebrated fifty years in the trade but it was cut short within the year by his early and unexpected death after only a few weeks of illness at the age of sixty-six.

The various St. John's newspapers paid tribute to Henley for his concern regarding his fellow human beings but principally for his entrepreneurship in founding the first mattress factory in Newfoundland. [16] But, undoubtedly, the best example of his entrepreneurship was the fact that he never incorporated but operated the factories in, and under, his own personal name and at his own personal risk. In fact the factories were never incorporated until after he had died. In what was perhaps a first for a Newfoundland female John J's widow, Catherine Henley, incorporated the business in 1944 and became the sole owner/operator. She appointed her son, Patrick, as the manager and her daughter, Catherine, as secretary. She continued to run the business until it closed its doors for good in the late nineteen fifties.

Patrick managed the business through the difficult years following World War II and suffered the misfortune of watching the business decay. Shortly after union with Canada the factory closed its doors for good. At this point it becomes necessary to account for its decease. Why did it eventually fail? In the case of the mattress factory it becomes a particularly intriguing question in view of its recognizable success for most of the years of its half-century operation. So what really brought an end to the great success story of John J. Henley?

---

[16]*Evening Telegram*, St. John's, 16, 18 Feb 1942; *Daily News*, St. John's, 16 Feb 1942.

In order to understand the ultimate failure of the mattress factory it is pertinent to take a close look at the reasons for its success in the first place. Henley was able to score a success in the factory's earliest beginnings because he knew the market well. He knew the demands of the cod and seal fisheries as well as the lumber camps. He was well known as an engaging personality and built a reputation as a type of man who knew every businessman by name. He understood the culture and was able to discern the trends that were taking place in the St. John's-led economy of Newfoundland. This was possible for a man like Henley because the market was so small. But those qualities in themselves do not guarantee success for if they did then there'd be no need of legislation, negotiations, treaties or even governments at all. For the crucial ingredient that allowed Henley to expand his product lines right up to the day he died and dominate the market was the fact that a government tariff shielded him from outside competition. When Canadian competition appeared following World War II, and especially after Confederation, the Henley factory faltered. And it faltered because the home market hadn't been big enough to allow Henley to expand to the size sufficient to withstand competition from larger factories on the mainland of Canada. So the Henley business eventually entered voluntary liquidation in 1957, through no inherent weakness in either Henley or his manufacturing process but simply through a weakness in the home market. Henceforward the bed market in Newfoundland would be supplied by Canadian and eventually American dealers.

Part II: Genealogy

Chapter One: Introduction.

British surname historians agree that the name Henley originated under local circumstances.[1] In other words the name was created from characteristics of the environment in their immediate geographic region. Surnames that originated in such a manner, for example, would be lake, meadow, lee, hill, etc, all emerging for obvious reasons as distinguishing characteristics amongst those who, heretofore, had borne but a single name.

While universal agreement exists on the general etymological origins of the Henley name there is some disagreement on the exact renderings. All agree that the name is derived from two words, one, 'hen' and the other 'ley'. Some say that the word hen is derived from the old English 'hind', meaning deer.[2] Others believe that it came from the old English habitation name, 'heah', for high, while still others believe it came from the old English word, 'henn' meaning hen, or wild bird.[3] As for the second part of the Henley name, ley, there is no dispute on the claim that it originated from the old English word, 'leah', meaning wood, clearing or pasture. There is a consensus then that the name Henley was an independent English creation

---

[1]Bardsley, Charles Wareing, **A Dictionary of English And Welsh Surnames** (Baltimore: Genealogical Publishing Company, 1968); Guppy, Henry Brougham, **Homes of Family Names in Great Britain** (London: Harrison And Sons, 1890); Hanks, Patrick and Hodges, Flavia, **A Dictionary of Surnames** (Oxford: Oxford University Press, 1989); Harrison, Harry, **Surnames Of The United Kingdom: A Concise Etymological Dictionary** (Baltimore: Genealogical Publishing Company, 1969).
[2]Ibid, 119.
[3]Hanks, 250.

going back to medieval times. That is good news for a genealogist, especially one tracing Henleys, but does it mean that all the Henleys of England belong, therefore, to one family tree? Possibilities based on logic and etymology raise serious doubts on this issue.

First of all, names created under local circumstances, like Henley, could easily be originated in different regions at the same time without reference to each other at all. That means that the Henley name could have been created simultaneously in Shropshire or Devon or in any county where clearings or pastures were found on a height of land. Complicating this problem is the claim by some that the Henley name is indeed Irish[4] and therefore some, or all, of the English Henleys could have originated in Ireland. A DNA project currently underway in England aimed at determining if all the English Henleys came from the one root will help towards resolving that difficulty.

In the meantime the quest for a continuous Henley line becomes even more challenging by virtue of the fact that by the end of the middle ages it has become a popular and fairly widely-distributed name. The first instance of the name was found under the variant, de Heneleg, in 1273 in County Salop.[5] Within a hundred years no fewer than four variants can be found in at least eight different counties. Eventually the name is found in almost every county of England

[4]Maclysaght, Edward, **The Surnames of Ireland, 3rd edn.** (Dublin: Irish Academic Press, 1978), 154; also Harrison, 199.
[5]While researching at the DRO in Exeter in 2006 I found an even earlier instance where a John de Henelegh owned a shop in Devon in 1263; see Reichel, Rev Oswald J, ed. **Feet Of Fines, vol I, Richard I – Henry III, 1196-1272** (Exeter: Devon and Cornwall record Society, 1912), 339-40.

and by the end of the 19th century it has
become so plentiful and famous that eleven
different Henley entries are found in the
national biographies of the United Kingdom.[6]
How, then, can one starting on a branch in
North America locate the correct Henley tree
in England? Thankfully, the oral traditions
on the Newfoundland branch have bloomed quite
luxuriantly.

There is a strong oral tradition
amongst the St. John's Henleys that their
ancestors, who were engaged in the West of
England-Newfoundland fisheries in the 18th
century, originated in County Devon. A quick
search of the International Genealogical
Index [7] affirms the credibility of that
contention. That source not only records the
popularity of the Henley name in Devon but
reveals it confined to the southern and
eastern half of the county. It was
prominently displayed in the hinterland of
the south coast ports that were heavily
involved in the Newfoundland trade. A further
concentrated and detailed search of the
records of one hundred and forty parishes in
that region shows that the Henley family was
centered in Newton Abbot from where they
branched out to the ports of Dartmouth,
Torquay and eventually St. John's.

[6]Stephen, Sir Leslie and Lee, Sir Sidney, **The Dictionary Of National Biography From The Earliest Times To 1900, vol IX** (Oxford: Oxford University Press, 1993); **The Concise Dictionary of National Biography From Earliest Times to 1985, vol II** (Oxford: Oxford University Press, 1992).
[7]The International Genealogical Index is an Internet service provided by the Church of Jesus Christ of Latter Day Saints, Salt Lake City, Utah, USA, who have made copies of English parish registers and made them available to researchers by means of the World Wide Web; hereafter I will refer to this source as IGI.

Newton Abbot, due to its importance in the Newfoundland trade[8], is a rather logical place in Devon where one would expect to discover Newfoundland roots. For from the earliest beginnings of the West Country fisheries that town has occupied a central place as a recruiting centre for personnel. In addition it was a market town which supplied numerous products for the Newfoundland trade. In 1850 White's *Devonshire Directory* described the town thus: "Newton Abbot ... is an ancient market town, picturesquely seated on the north side of the small river Lemon, near its confluence with the navigable river Teign, 15 miles S. by W. of Exeter,... It has now about 3000 inhabitants; exclusive of its suburb of Newton Bushel . . . The town has many good houses and shops, especially in the new streets laid out during the last ten years".[9] Thus it was admirably situated to carry on business relating to the maritime trades.

Of those Newton Abbot personnel who engaged in commerce in that favored location the name of Henley is perhaps the most prominent. From the English records that have survived it is clear that not only do Henleys have an ancient lineage dating back to pre-Reformation times in Devon but were a distinguished family as early as 1543. In that year Walter Hendley[10] was appointed as one of the Commissioners to sell both

---

[8]Handcock, **Soe longe...**, 63, 147, 156-8, 163, 166, 168-71, 174-5, 179, 181-3, 254, 262.
[9]**Devon Gazetteer**: Newton Abbott.
[10]In the earliest records the name appears as Hendly/Hendley, Endly/Endley and sometimes as Endle; over time it evolved through Henly into its modern form of Henley.

monastic and other crown lands in Devon [11].
When the parish records came into being the
Henley name appeared regularly in the
parishes of south Devon and it became
possible to trace a continuous Henley family
line from 16th century Devon down to the 21st
century in St. John's.

Before we embark on the history of a
family tree reconstructed from the Devon
parish registers it is wise to determine the
exact status and character of the English
church records. Church recordings of baptisms,
marriages and burials did not begin in
England until 1538 when the first law
requiring such was enacted. At first the
churches did not comply and for many years
thereafter there are no such records for many
parishes all over England. In 1558 the
government initiated a serious effort to
force churches to comply with the law but it
still took many years to create a uniform
practice throughout the country. The result
is that we cannot expect to find a complete
record of any parish from the time of the
original compulsory legislation in 1538. For
example, of the 621 parishes for which there
are records in the Devon Record Office at
Exeter only 206 have baptisms, marriages or
burials which pre-date 1600. As well the
ravages of time, damage from the elements,
floods, fires, wars and rebellions have all
combined to create gaps in what would
otherwise be excellent sources for baptisms,
marriages and burials. The records in the
old parish of Abbotskerswell, for example,
start in 1607 but for some years only five
or six baptisms have survived and for
sporadic years there are none at all; not one

---

[11]Youings, Joyce, ed, **Devon Monastic Lands: Calendar Of Particulars For Grants 1536-1558**, (Torquay: Devon & Cornwall Record Society, 1955), XIII.

entry has survived for the years 1665-68 incl, none for 1673-5, and the years from 1682-1687 inclusive are completely blank.

For Tormoham, an ancient parish now included in the boundaries of Torquay, the first records are for the year 1612 but for the decades following they are few and far between; there are none at all for the years 1633-5, only one page of baptisms, marriage's and burial's for 1636; none between 1636 and 1664, and sporadic years are missing up to the end of the century; only after 1700 is there a continuous record of baptisms, marriages and burials.

In addition to the above problems there is the added difficulty of attempting to read entries that are several hundred years old. The wear and tear of the ages plus the fact that one must read microfilm copies, some times renders the task of deciphering quite impossible. Then there is the problem of lack of consistency in the formation of letters, the minute form of some handwritten entries and the near illegibility of others. In Bow, for example, although records begin in 1598, yet from that date to 1674 there are only eleven worn and unreadable leaves of baptisms, marriages and burials. For that parish the only readable entries for the entire 17th century are those for 1688. The task of researching the English parish records can be so daunting that one could spend hours attempting to decipher just one page. Even for entries that are typed (of which there are a few such transcriptions) the task of reading those for hundreds of parishes on microfilm can consume an extensive period of time.

There are other issues that seriously impact the study of English genealogy that have nothing to do with either the survival rate or the material quality of the parish

registers. Up to 1754 only basic information
was recorded for baptisms, marriages and
burials. That means that in the baptismal
records before that date you can simply
expect to find the name of the child and the
father. In fact in several instances the
officiating minister just merely listed the
names of the children baptized and gave no
other information at all. Of all the records,
perhaps the burial ones are the least helpful
for only the name of the deceased plus the
date of burial are registered. As given names
were frequently repeated in family lines, the
genealogist can have great difficulty in
identifying the deceased. Thankfully, in 1754,
they began to record the names of witnesses
and signatures to marriages. In the same year
it also became compulsory that one of the
parties to the marriage must reside in the
parish where the wedding was taking place.
Afterwards it became the tradition to perform
the marriage in the bride's home parish. But
it wasn't until 1813 that the father's
occupation and abode were added to the
baptisms and age and abode added to burials.
In 1837 age, abode plus father's name and
occupation were added to the marriages.

Having given consideration to all of
the above I decided to adopt a strategy for
my study of the Henley genealogy through the
English parish registers that would be
efficient, reliable and economical at the
same time. Such a strategy was rendered
necessary not only by the circumstances
surrounding the microfilm copies of the
parish registers themselves but also by the
fact that copies of such registers are also
available on the internet through courtesy of
the Church of Jesus Christ Of Latter Day
Saints. That church, for theological reasons,
has been microfilming church and census
records, world-wide, for depository in their

library at Salt Lake City. They have uploaded many of their copies to the internet and the chief feature of the latter's genealogical resources is their International Genealogical Index (IGI). Here one can view typed copies of all baptisms or marriages from a particular Devon parish going back in some instances to the beginning of the parish records in the 16th century. The question which immediately arises is: why spend endless hours poring over microfilm copies of almost illegible parish registers when one can use the IGI? The answer is not only a complex one but exceedingly crucial for the study of genealogy.

In the first place the Latter Day Saints never received permission from the Church in Devon to microfilm the original records. Instead they resorted to filming *copies* that had already been made. Therefore whatever mistakes had been made in the copies being filmed were simply repeated by the microfilming. Again the IGI does not encompass the total number of parish registers which remain extant in Devon and from those that have been filmed the burials have been excluded. Thus, the point to remember is that the parish records that have been filmed are not complete. More worrisome is the fact that all such records made by the LDS have been transcribed in type form in order to be loaded to the internet. During those transcriptions one must allow for numerous errors especially since the computer creates opportunities for making errors. One such example from the IGI is as follows: their baptismal records for the Salem Independent Chapel at Newton Abbot show that a Richard Henley was christened there to William and Marie on 29th June 1645, but my detailed and careful search of the records showed that on 29th June Richard was christened in the parish of Abbotskerswell just outside Newton Abbot. As a result of errors like that, the Devon Family History Society has issued a stern warning to all researchers to use the IGI with extreme caution.

For the reasons outlined above I approached the IGI with a particular strategy in mind. First, I relied on the IGI only for parish records that could not be obtained here in St. John's. Secondly, I used the remainder as a guide only, which means that I referred to the IGI merely as an indicator of name distribution. Generally speaking, if the IGI search of a particular parish showed no instance of a Henley name or any of its variations in a three hundred-year span of baptisms and marriages, then I concluded that it would be a waste of time to pursue a detailed search of that parish's registers at the Maritime History Archives.[12] Nevertheless, I made exceptions to this rule in cases where I was in need of a missing baptismal or marriage record. If an adjacent parish existed for which the IGI had failed to locate a Henley I performed a detailed search of that particular parish in order to eliminate the possibility that at least one such record had been missed by the IGI transcribers. One such example relates to the Torquay area. Having searched the films of the registers for both the old Torquay parishes of Tormoham and St. Marychurch I was still in need of additional information relating to certain marriages. I did an IGI search of the neighboring Brixham parishes and when my questions were not conclusively answered I decided to do a personal, first-hand search and carefully perused the Brixham

---

[12]The Maritime History Archives are located at Memorial University.

registers at the Maritime History Archives,
St. John's.

The Maritime History Archives at
Memorial University is one of the most
outstanding sources in North America for the
study of English and Irish genealogy. There I
found copies of baptismal, marriage and
burial records from four hundred and thirty-
four (434) parishes out of a maximum seven
hundred and forty-seven (747) from Devon. [13]
From a Newfoundland perspective this must be
considered a rather comprehensive coverage of
Newfoundland family source areas in that
county. It means that approximately 75% of
all Devon parishes can be researched at the
Maritime History Archives. In addition to
what has been said earlier about the state of
those records and the difficulties of reading
them on microfilm[14] I wish to point out that
as a general rule I did not study the burial
records. Those records yielded so little
information I decided to concentrate on
baptismal and marriage records instead,
resorting only to the burials when I needed
assistance in confirming a possible death.
With those considerations in mind let us now
take a look at the Newton Abbot Henleys and
their main branches in Dartmouth, Torquay and
Newfoundland.

---

[13] It must be remembered that one hundred and thirty-eight of that total
were created in the post-1850 period.
[14] MHA also carries a small collection of manuscript copies of some
Devon parish records and the QEII Library also has the published
registers from nine Devon parishes.

Chapter Two

The Newton Abbot Henleys

Although most of the marriage and baptismal entries for the Henleys at the root of this family tree are located in the parish of Abbotskerswell, for a number of reasons I am adopting the practice of referring to them as the Newton Abbot Henleys. First, oral tradition in the Henley family has always maintained Newton Abbot as their ancestral home. Secondly, Abbotskerswell is just a small village on the southern border of the better known market town of Newton Abbot, famous for its historical connections to Newfoundland. Thirdly, by the early years of the 18th century almost all the descendants of the early Abbotskerswell Henleys had relocated to Wolborough Parish in Newton Abbot.

The earliest marriage entry of a Henley in the parish records of the Newton Abbot area occurs in 1614 when Luke Henley is married to Agnes Erven in the parish of Abbotskerswell[1]. Henceforward there is an easily identifiable, continuous Henley family line that eventually branched out to the ports of Dartmouth and Torquay in Devon and to Carbonear and St. John's in Newfoundland. There is an earlier Henley entry, however, in the city of Exeter in 1573[2]. That was a marriage of Edward Hendlye to Margarette Periam in January of that year, and there followed a number of Henley entries in the parish records of the several parishes in and

---

[1]The oldest Henley entry of all in the Newton Abbot region is a 1607 burial in Abbotskerswell of Henry Henley.
[2]St. John's, MHA: Exeter, St. Sidwell, Marriages 21 Jan 1573.

around the city of Exeter for the next three centuries. Why, then, would not the Exeter Henleys form the base of the Henley tree in place of Newton Abbot? The answer is a rather simple one. Although the city of Exeter became the location for numerous Henley marriages in the 16th and 17th centuries, there is no continuous Henley line whatsoever in that area. In fact the records show eight Henley marriages in the Exeter parishes between 1573 and 1688, yet there were only five Henley baptisms in that entire one hundred and fifteen year period. It appears that Exeter, a busy port on the navigable river Exe, served as the capital and also as a source of eligible brides for mariners frequenting that port. As well Exeter was the seat of the Devon diocese and many of the visiting sailors and mariners were happy to have that ceremony performed in the capital. Numerous Henleys married in the capital yet they neither settled nor reared their children there. A good example is Samuel Henley, a master mariner who was engaged in the foreign going trades[3]. Samuel was born in Abbotskerswell in 1719, operated frequently out of Exeter and married Elizabeth Venning at St. Peter's cathedral there in 1744. Samuel and Elizabeth, however, reared all their children in Newton Abbot where Samuel died and was buried in 1789. Thus, I will not consider Exeter to have originated any Henley tree and will continue to consider that the Henleys originated in Newton Abbot.[4]

---

[3]Below, 115.

[4]Besides, a prominent citizen of Exeter mentioned in his diary in 1635 that his neighbours, the Henleys, had come from across the border in Somerset: see Westcountry Studies Library, Exeter, T N Brushfield, "The Financial Diary of A Citizen Of Exeter, 1631-1643" in **Transactions of the Devonshire Association, vol. XXXIII** (Plymouth: The Devonshire Association, 1901), 201.

Similar remarks apply to Otis Henley
who began a Henley family line in Paignton,
near Torquay, in 1580. With a brief
interruption in the late 1580's, that line
continued down to 1622 after which date they
all completely disappeared. And a thorough
search of all the surrounding parishes in the
region confirmed that the Henley line did not
reappear in the Torquay area until 1741, at
which time it can be clearly identified as an
offshoot of the Newton Abbot tree[5].

Luke's marriage to Agnes Erven in 1614,
to which we referred above, notes that he was
"son of John" while the burial records of
1619 note that on Mar 1 there was buried
"John Henley an old man". As I consider that
anyone over fifty years of age, at that time,
would be considered "old", I am therefore
estimating that John would have been born
around 1559. Although the pertinent baptismal
record did not survive I am confident that
John was indeed the father of the Luke that
married Agnes Erven. My Henley family tree
will therefore show John as the original root
in this region.

At the time of Luke's marriage there
are only two other Henley contemporaries who
could qualify as Luke's siblings. One was
Willmet Henley who had an illegitimate
daughter, Thomasyne, in 1618. Neither one of
them ever appear in the records again. The
other was Richard Henley who had John
Bickford christened in Abbotskerswell in 1623[6].
I am concluding that there is quite a strong
likelihood that Richard and Thomasyne were
the brother and sister, respectively, of Luke.
Nevertheless, this is not of much consequence

---

[5]Below, Chapter IV.
[6]A Richardus Henley married Maria Lambert in 1641 at Ashburton, just
6-7miles (10-12 kms) from Abbotskerswell and it is quite possible that
he was Richard's son, too, but there was no issue from that marriage.

for the family tree because they and their descendants soon disappear entirely from the records either though death or emigration. It therefore fell to Luke to perpetuate the Henley line.

Luke and Agnes had three sons and one daughter. The one daughter, Mary, did not survive the first year of her birth and brother John, apparently, never married. But sons Luke Jr [7] and William originated substantial families. Luke's marriage record has not survived but I am assuming he married in Wolborough[8], Newton Abbot for his children, Luke III, Luce and Andrew, were christened there in 1642, 1645 and 1655 respectively. Luke III, whose marriage record has not survived either, had one son in 1688 who, in turn, was named Luke. Perhaps this was a late marriage because Luke III was then forty-six years of age and that would account for the small family. In turn Luke IV married around 1720 and had a son christened at Wolborough in 1723. Luke IV named his only son, not surprisingly, Luke. For three generations this branch of the Henley tree had been hanging by a thread, having passed through three Lukes in a row. But there it ended for Luke V disappeared from the records entirely and either through death or emigration this branch of the Henleys came to a close.

Luke III's brother, Andrew, however, who married Dunes Thorne at Wolborough in 1687, was much more prolific. He had at last three sons, Luke, John and Edward of whom only John married. He married Mary Wills in 1722 but the marriage produced only one child, John Jr, and the burial records reveal that

---

[7]There are so many Lukes at this time that for ease of tracking them we will designate them as Luke Sr, Jr, III, IV, etc
[8]Wolborough is one of the two ancient parishes comprising Newton Abbott; the other one is Highweek.

both were dead by 1728. One would think initially that the line had ended there but in Churston Ferrers, just a few miles south of Newton Abbot, there is a marriage in 1721 of Andrew Henley "of Woolboro" and I am concluding that it is quite logical to place him on the Henley tree as the son of Andrew and Dunes Thorn. Andrew Jr's wife was Mary Cole and in Wolborough they had two sons, Luke and John. Luke later settled in Torquay and we shall return to him later when we relate the story of the Torquay Henleys. John, however, had a most interesting life which we cannot fail to recount.

John lived at home until he was about eleven years old at which time he was apprenticed to a yeoman in Stokeinteignhead. He worked there for almost eleven years following which, having reached the age of twenty-one, he went out to work in the Newfoundland fisheries. He fished there perhaps for the usual term of one summer-two winters and returned to Devon. Once again he bound himself to a yeoman farmer and lived the life of an agricultural laborer. He drifted around for several years performing the very difficult labor required by farming families at that time. At times he is found in Stokeinteignhead, then Teignmouth and latterly Chudleigh where he settled down long enough to marry Alice Berry. There he had one son, John Jr, before he once again moved to Stokeinteignhead. John Jr married Mary Martin and had two daughters and three sons. Only one of those three sons, Richard, married. He married Mary Bowden and had two children but only one son, Thomas, to carry on the Henley line. Thomas became a farm laborer like his direct ancestors and in the 1851 census we find him as a servant to George Bond in Bishopsteignton. But he is nowhere to be found in the later 19th century English census

records leaving us to believe that he either
died or emigrated. Thus the line that had
begun with 'Chudleigh' John's marriage to
Alice Berry in 1757 had died out by the
middle of the 19th century in England. Because
the family line begun by Chudleigh John's
only two, male, first cousins had already
died out in the 18th century, [9] it means that
the once-extensive branches originated by
Luke Jr, (b.1618), had all come to an end. We
will therefore continue the Newton Abbot
story by returning to the only one of Luke
Jr's siblings we have not yet met, viz:
William.

William, b.1620, married Marie[10] Osborne
in 1643 and had one daughter and three sons.
Of the four only Richard and John married.
John's marriage record did not survive but
the baptism of his son, Thomas, in 1691
reveals his wife's name as Elizabeth.
Unfortunately Elisabeth died in 1707 leaving,
it appears, Thomas as the only offspring but
the records indicate that John married again.
In 1709 there is a baptism in Abbotskerswell
of a male child, John, "son of John", and
John, the widower, is the only possibility as
the child's father. John Jr. in turn married
Ann Curyer in 1738 but no children issued
from that marriage. His step-brother, Thomas,
however, had much better luck. He married
Jane Martyne in 1720 and had seven children.
Nevertheless this branch of the Henley tree
was destined to die out by the end of the
century. That occurred mainly because five of
Thomas's seven children were females and a
sixth, Peter, died in infancy. The remaining
offspring was named Thomas who, in 1748,
married Margaret Studdy at Teigngrace. They

---

[9]See family tree, chapter VII.
[10]Her name is originally spelled Mare in the marriage record but in the
baptismal records it soon adopts the modern form.

had three daughters whose baptisms are shown
in the records and one would normally expect
the line to end here. However, the Muster
Rolls[11] of 1790 show that there was a Thomas
Henley of Abbotskerswell serving on board the
schooner, **Fortitude**, involved in the
Newfoundland trade. His age is given as
thirty-nine placing his birth date in 1751
approximately. That would fit exactly with
his being a son of Thomas and Margaret Studdy
and I am therefore placing him in the family
tree as such. Although Thomas took a wife,
only one child issued from the marriage. That
was a daughter, Grace, born in 1787. Thus,
this branch of the Henley tree came to a
close. Let us retrace our steps now, back
through three Thomas's to John, the son of
William and Marie, to determine if John's
brother, Richard, produced any offspring.

Richard was much older than John,
having been born at Abbotskerswell in 1645
and was eligible for marriage when John was
but a child. No marriage for Richard appears
in the Abbotskerswell parish registers, yet
the baptismal records show christenings for
him there in 1670 and 1673. That is perfectly
consistent with his having been married
sometime between 1663 and 1669, and the
missing marriage record is also consistent
with practices current at that time as well
as the culture of record keeping outlined in
chapter one. However, at the same time there
appeared in Dartmouth a record relating to
the Henleys for the very first time in the
history of that port. That was a marriage in
1668 at Townstall, of Richard Henley to Mary
Roads and at this moment in the Henley
history a dilemma arises. Is this the same

---

[11]Unless otherwise indicated references to Muster Rolls and other
shipping records come from the Keith Matthews Fonds at the Maritime
History Archives, Memorial University.

Henley as the Richard at Abbotskerswell? The question is transformed into a double dilemma with the marriage in 1707 of William Henley at Abbotskerswell to Ann Churchwell. There is no baptismal record for William and his probable birth in the 1680's places him right in the midst of the dilemma surrounding Richard. I like to refer to William as "the famous William Henley" for a variety of reasons. First, he and Ann gave birth to eight children, the largest Henley family since the beginning of this family tree in 1559. Secondly, he and his sons originated extensive family branches that blossomed in Dartmouth and Torquay; and, thirdly, he is the man from whom descended, without challenge, the Henley family line that flourishes in St. John's today. His identity is therefore most crucial for this particular study.

In the pre-1690 period there are only four sets of parents having children in parishes within, and bordering, Newton Abbot and it is obvious that one of them gave birth to the famous William. The four eligible fathers therefore, according to the records, are Andrew, b. 1655, Luke III, b. 1642, John, b.1659 and Richard, b. 1645. Selecting the correct father is simply a matter of choice based on reason. Andrew must be eliminated because his marriage did not take place until August 1687 and his son, Luke, baptized in August, 1688, was therefore his first child. That means that the earliest possible date for William's birth in this family would be the end of June, 1689. As William was married in early February, 1707 it would mean a marriage when he was five months short of his eighteenth birthday. As I have never found a marriage earlier than an eighteenth birthday in the four hundred years of Henley genealogy I am ruling it out here and looking to the other three possibilities for William's parents.

Luke III, b.1642, could well have been the father of William for he was having children by 1688[12] and, given his age, could easily have been married anytime before 1680. But in that particular family, as we have seen above, both Luke and his brother, Andrew kept alive the tradition of naming Lukes amongst their offspring and Luke appears unfailingly in their descendant trees until 1759. Now William, as we have indicated, had the largest Henley family in more than a hundred years and never gave the name Luke to any of his sons. Nor did the name appear in his extensive clan of grandsons and for that reason I am not willing to consider that Luke III was William's father.

John, b. 1659 and Richard, b. 1645 are now the only remaining possibilities for the father of William and we must make a choice between them. As it is not possible to have one hundred percent certainty on this question we will make our selection based simply on reason. There really isn't much consequence for choosing the one over the other for, given the fact that John and Richard are brothers, neither the ancestral nor descendant tree would change. After much deliberation I have decided to favor John as the father of William.

Now that we have made a conclusion about the identity of William let us return to the dilemma surrounding Richard, himself, and discover why he must be eliminated as the possible father of William. As we have learned from our studies to date, the parish registers of Abbotskerswell contain no marriage for Richard although the baptismal register records the following christenings

---

[12]Above, 104-5; see also family tree.

there: in 1670 of Hannah Henley "daughter of Richard"; in 1673 of Elizabeth Henley "daughter of Richard". A search of the records of all the parishes in the entire region of south and east Devon revealed a marriage in Townstall, Dartmouth in 1668 of Richard Endly and Mary Roads. Although Dartmouth parish records have survived from 1586 that is the first mention ever of the name Endly/Henley in the baptisms, marriages or burials. I do not consider that occurrence to be a simple coincidence for Mary Roads/Rhodes was baptized there in May, 1641 and it is logical to conclude that Richard of Abbotskerswell married in his bride's home town. Dartmouth is only 9-10 miles (approx.16 kms) down the road from Abbotskerswell and such a move for a Newton Abbot area resident must be considered a logical one given their respective positions in the sea-going trades[13]. The dates of the baptized children also add credence to the view that there was only one Richard. There are no baptisms in the Dartmouth records for any of Richard's children following the 1668 marriage date, but Abbotskerswell records one in 1670 and another in 1673, perfectly consistent with the marriage date as well as the fact that Richard and Mary settled in Richard's home village of Abbotskerswell. In addition the Dartmouth parish registers show baptisms for Richard's children in 1674, 1676, 1678, 1682 and 1686. Those are the happenings that gave rise to the original question regarding the possibility of the two Richards. However, while those baptismal recordings were being made in Dartmouth none occur for Richard in the parish registers of Abbotskerswell. That

---

[13]Handcock, **Soe longe** ..., especially pp. 59, 62- 63, 65, 81-2, 146-7,154-170 etc.

would be consistent with Richard having taken up residence in Dartmouth.

In attempting to resolve the problem of whether or not there were two Richards I checked and double-checked all the available records, including the copies of original registers and Bishops Transcripts, as well as the modern transcriptions. The latter were typed transcripts made in 1958 in Devon by Mrs. G. H. Smith of the Devon and Cornwall Record Society and I thought that I had proven that there were indeed two Richards, one in Abbotskerswell and one in Dartmouth, when I found an entry in the Wolborough parish records for a baptism of Margaret Henley, "daughter of Richard", 1 June 1676. You will recall that Richard had earlier had a daughter Marie baptized in Dartmouth on 31 Jan 1676 and, on the surface, it would seem that the case was closed against an only Richard. But I felt aprehensive about Mrs. Smith's entry because following the notation of Margaret's baptism Mrs. Smith wrote the following in brackets, "on first page of baptism". In other words, the entry had been made out of chronological order thereby giving rise to serious doubts about when the child had actually been born. I forthwith double-checked the Bishops Transcripts. Those had begun in 1598 when it became compulsory for Ministers to forward copies of their registers to the Bishop of the diocese. Known as Bishops Transcripts they have been microfilmed and copies are available at the MHA. But those transcripts carried no such baptismal entry for Margaret. Then what about the possibility that the parish clergy, in copying their 1676 registers, made a mistake and overlooked Margaret? Thus, I hired a genealogist in Exeter who checked the original registers but could not find the entry from which Mrs. Smith made her copy. (A few years later, on visiting Exeter, I enjoyed the opportunity of checking those originals myself and for 1653 there was no such entry, and the same was true for 1676). While that does not prove it never existed, it is rather unconvincing evidence on which to base a conclusion that there were two Richards [14] . I will therefore persist in treating Richard of Abbotskerswell and Dartmouth as the same man who reared some of his family in Abbotskerswell and then, following 1673, moved permanently to Dartmouth. As the parish register of 1707 carried the note that both William and his bride Ann Churchwell were "of Abbotskerswell", then I am forced to eliminate Richard as William's father, leaving John as the sole possibility. As Richard had moved to Dartmouth where he established a permanent and extensive branch of the Henley tree I will therefore resume the discussion of him and his descendants in the next chapter under the Dartmouth Henleys. As we have now formed a conclusion regarding William's identity let us return to Richard's brother, John, whose son, Thomas, will now have an older brother, William, not shown in the records.

A survey of the marriages from this entire period reveals that the great majority of male marriages occurred within the 10-year range beginning at the eighteenth birthday. William therefore was most likely born some time between 1679 and 1687. Because the baptismal records for Abbotskerswell are missing for the period from 1682-1687, inclusive, I am concluding that those years

---

[14]There is also the possibility that the entry from which Mrs. Smith made her copy was really an abbreviated "Margt" and could well have been really Marie for whom there had been a private baptism in Dartmouth in January and a more public one in Wolborough in June; that was not an uncommon occurrence.

contain the most likely dates for William's birth and, as he had a large family, I will conclude that he was born in 1687 making him approximately twenty years of age when he married Ann Churchwell in 1707. That marriage produced two girls and six boys. Ann, b.1710, died before her second birthday while the other girl, Elizabeth, never married but had an illegitimate son, Philip Ball Henley, in 1748 and a second one, John, in 1752. Of the six boys, Samuel died in infancy while the other five married and had thirty-nine children between them. Richard, b. 1716, married a woman from Torquay and settled there to begin a rather large branch of the Newton Abbot Henleys. We shall deal with them later in chapter IV as the Torquay Henleys. The other four brothers reared their families in the Newton Abbot area.

One of the four brothers was William, a man whose birth/baptismal record has not survived. But as he married in Abbotskerswell in 1731 I have judged him to be the son of William and Ann. Based on a study of the baptismal dates of his brothers and sisters and taking the date of his marriage into account I am estimating his birth to have taken place in 1708. William Jr. married Alice Oxneham (aka Oxenham) and had five daughters and one son. I have not been successful in finding marriages for any of them. The parish registers of Kingskerswell record a marriage there of Elizabeth Henley in 1771 to Peter Yabsley. As Kingskerswell was only about five miles away it might be reasonable to conclude that this was the thirty-year-old Elizabeth, daughter of William and Alice. But Elizabeth had a younger first cousin, age twenty-one and it would be just as reasonable to conclude it was the latter. As for the only son in this family, William, b.1743, he may have married in Abbotskerswell for there is a son, John, baptized to him there in 1774. However, there are no other children for William appearing in the records in the succeeding twenty-five years and this branch may have died out unless the John who had a daughter, Elizabeth, in Newton Abbot in 1798 is indeed William's son. That is difficult to say from our vantage point for no marriage has been discovered for John and Elizabeth and no other children appear in the records for them. The only evidence pointing to John as William's son is the fact that he was rearing a family in Newton Abbot, only about one mile from Abbotskerswell. However, it is possible that the entire family of William and Alice emigrated, either to another part of England or to the New World. With the limited evidence available to us we will have to leave it unresolved for the time being.

John, b. 1728, became an important figure in the community as he served as churchwarden for his parish. He reared a family of at least nine children, two of whom were males. According to the parish records William was the only son to marry and as he settled in Torquay we shall take up his story later in Chapter IV under the Torquay Henleys. However, in the Abbotskerswell registers for 1783 there appears a marriage of Richard Henley and Mary Codner. From the range of possibilities I have concluded that the only possible parents for Richard are John, who married Mary Rodd in 1758, and Samuel who married an unknown Mary c.1755[15]. The Board of Trade records show that Richard was alternating with William Henley as captain of

[15]I am excluding the Richard, b. 1761 to Edward and Mary, because his marriage record to Joan Creed said he belonged to Highweek.

the **Eliza**[16] in 1810-11 and in the latter year William's age is given as thirty-six and identified as "of Abbotskerswell" but now living in Torquay. I am identifying this William as the one born to John and Mary at Abbotskerswell in 1774 and will therefore conclude that the Richard who married Mary Codner is William's brother and son of John and Mary Rodd. Richard and Mary Codner had at least three sons, but as they all settled in Torquay we shall finish their story later in chapter IV as the Torquay Henleys.

The remaining two sons of William and Ann Churchwell, Samuel and Edward, originated extensive branches of the Henley family tree in Newton Abbot. Samuel seems to have been the first of his line to be involved in the Newfoundland trade. He became a master mariner and eventually took possession of the 110-ton **Britannia** trading between the various Devon ports, St. John's and the West Indies. The **Britannia** was a sack ship with two decks and had a 12-ft. draught. Samuel was very probably freighting goods and supplies to and from his son's firms in Wolboro and St. John's.

Samuel married Elizabeth Venning at St. Peter's Cathedral in Exeter in 1744 and reared a family of six children in Newton Abbot. One of them, Elizabeth, b.1748, died shortly afterwards and the next girl, b. 1750, was given her name. I am concluding that she was the one who married Peter Yabsley in 1771 at nearby Kingskerswell. She had a first cousin, Elizabeth, b. 1741 at Newton Abbot and she could well have been the one who married Yabsley but, as it is simply a matter of guessing, I will choose the younger woman. And nothing appears in the records for John.

---

[16]The **Eliza** was owned by their first cousin, William, son of their uncle Edward; below, 119.

John's brothers, Samuel Jr, b.1744 and
William, b.1746 were heavily involved in the
Newfoundland trade. William first shows up in
the shipping records as captain of a schooner
belonging to John Noble of Dartmouth. Within
a few years the shipping records describe
Samuel and William as "merchants of Wolboro"
and by the mid-1780's they are owners of the
Jane and the **Hazard**. The **Hazard** was a single-
decked, 120-ton, sheathed brig with beams.
She carried a 10-ft. draught when fully
loaded and plied between Dartmouth and
Newfoundland ports. There are several
references in the shipping and Colonial
Office records to William Henley carrying on
business in St. John's in the 1770's down to
the post-1800 period[17]. From my study of the
Henley family tree I have concluded that the
Henley in question is William, b.1746, son of
Samuel and brother of Samuel Jr. Aaron Graham,
who came to St. John's in 1779 as secretary
to Governor Richard Edwards, found William
Henley already carrying on a fishery when he
arrived. By 1784 William is identified as one
of the principal inhabitants in St. John's
and from 1786 to 1789 serves on the grand
jury. The same classification can be applied
to his brother, Samuel, who by 1777 has
become the grand jury foreman. A 1788 record
shows William as a house owner and one for
1791 lists him as a merchant of St. John's.
And a 1794 record shows brother Samuel as
owner of a house in St. John's as well. In
other words, from the scanty records we have
available we can tell that William and Samuel
have business operations both in St. John's
and Wolboro and are quite probably splitting
their time living between the two places as
was quite common in that period. By 1795 the

---

[17]St. John's, MHA: Matthews Name Files (MNF), "William Henley";
also CO 194/11, 409; C O 194/35, 276; vol 38; CO 324/27.

Wolboro branch of the business is bankrupt but William is still carrying on a fishery in St. John's and supplying planters as well. But by 1799 the latter business was forced into insolvency as well. In the post-1800 period there are varying references to business operations in the St. John's area under the names of William Henley, William C. Henley and William Charles Henley. But insufficient information prevents us from making a positive identification as to which particular William is involved.

William's marriage record did not survive and the baptismal records of their children identify the mother as Joanna. However, there is a marriage record in the St. John's Church of England parish registers dated Sept 8, 1779 for William Henley and Joan Moore. It seems reasonable to conclude that this is the missing marriage and that William Henley and Joan Moore are the William and Joanna appearing in the baptismal records of Wolborough. Nevertheless serious doubt is cast on this judgment by the fact that their first child was baptized at Newton Abbot in April 1779 while the marriage did not take place until five months later in St. John's. William and Joanna reared nine children in Newton Abbot between 1779 and 1796, one of whom was William, b.1781. As there is a marriage in Kingskerswell in 1800 of William Henley and Jane Creed it poses a problem as to which William is the correct one for there was another William, b. 1764, living nearby. Perhaps their respective ages would tend to point to the younger William but this is not sufficient evidence on which to base a definitive conclusion. Nevertheless, I will favor the younger William and consider Jane Creed to have married the son of William and Joanna because the marriage register referred

to her husband as "of Wolborough" [18] . And
although Edward and Mary, who were the
parents of the other William, had all their
children baptized at the Salem Independent
chapel in Newton Abbot, they remained
domiciled in Abbotskerswell. The records
though yield no information as to any
offspring of William's marriage to Jane, and
in fact William's entire family of eight
siblings poses somewhat of a mystery. That is
because they seem to have disappeared
altogether from the baptismal, marriage and
census records. By 1826 one of them, Maria,
was living in Devonport and another, Mary was
in Guernsey. It is likely that the remainder
emigrated as well.

Edward, b.1730, the youngest child of
William Henley and Ann Churchwell, married
Mary Garret in 1757 at Abbotskerswell and
became an important figure in the economy of
Devon and Newfoundland. He established a
mercantile firm at Newton Abbot and St.
John's that became involved in every branch
of the West Country fisheries. He owned
several properties in Newton Abbot,
Abbotskerswell and St. John's. He was also
the owner of at least one schooner. In St.
John's he was a householder and an important
figure in the political life of the town as
well. Throughout the 1770's he served for a
number of years on the grand jury in that
seaport town. When he died at Newton Abbot in
1806 he left substantial estates to his
family. He decreed that his wife Mary should
live the remainder of her life rent free in
the ancestral home and granted her a lifetime
annuity of fifty pounds. To son John he left
a tenement called Rainsey's in Wolborough

---

[18]"Devonshire Parish Registers: Marriages, I", **Phillimore Parish
Register Series**, vol. CXIL (London: Phillimore & Co. 1909), 37.

plus an estate in East Ogwell. He also left to John an estate in Wolborough composed of a barn and three fields known separately as Broomdown, Mocerd Park and the Peace Parks. He even left twenty pounds each to two of his grandsons, and to sons Richard and John, "all the residue" of his estates. That may have been an indication that his other children, for whom I could not find marriages, were deceased.

Edward Henley and Mary Garrett reared one daughter, Elizabeth, and five sons, John, Edward, Samuel, William and Richard all of whom followed up their father's connection with Newfoundland. Even daughter Elizabeth was part owner of the house in St. John's. I have not been successful in finding marriages for Edward, b.1759, Elizabeth, b.1759 or Samuel b. 1769. There was a marriage at Kingskerswell in 1800 of a William Henley to Jane Creed who just might be the son of Edward and Mary. However, for the reasons given above I am concluding it was the younger William. Nevertheless, this is of little consequence as no offspring resulted from that marriage. Even so, William, Edward's son, was an important figure in the Newfoundland trade operating out of Newton Abbot. By his early twenties he was captain of the **Friendship**, trading between the Devon ports of Torquay and Plymouth to Cape Broyle and St. John's. He established himself in the shipping business by acquiring ownership of the schooner, **Eliza**. She was a single-decked schooner with beams and in 1793 and 1795 he had her repaired and enlarged. She carried a 10-ft. draught and plied regularly between the south Devon ports and Newfoundland. In 1793 William showed up in the Muster Rolls as a merchant and was supplying planters in St. John's. By 1795 he had recruited his first cousin, William, from Abbotskerswell to be captain of the **Eliza** and was paying more attention to the supplying business. In the post-1795 period William expanded his field of operations to include Ireland and the Mediterranean.

By the turn of the century William's brother, Edward, may have taken the place of his father, Edward Sr, in the business. In the post-1800 period there are at least three Edwards, if not four, involved in the economic life of St. John's. With the limited records available it is not possible to sort them out correctly.

William's brother, Samuel, b.1769, appears not to have married yet he too was involved in the Newfoundland trade. He started out as a seaman working on vessels owned by his brother, Richard. Eventually he formed a partnership with Richard and owned the schooner **Aurora**.

William's brother, John, was perhaps more heavily involved in the Newfoundland trade than were his brothers. The few reports that have survived from the shipping records of the 1790's indicate that there was a John Henley operating a business in St. John's at that time. He appears to be connected to a William Henley and his wife is living in Newton Bushel. Those pieces of evidence point to John, William's brother, son of Edward and Mary. In St. John's his business appears to be managed by one, George Burton. By the 1820's those same records identify a John Henley, merchant of St. John's, who has formed a partnership with John B Bland and owns a fleet of schooners such as the **Jane**, the **Margaret**, the **Rob Roy**, the **Three Sisters** and the **Elizabeth**. But as there were other John Henleys involved in the Newfoundland trade at that time, specifically from Dartmouth, we are unable to make positive identifications regarding Bland's partner.

Surviving records indicate, though, that it was a John Henley from London.

John married Sarah Bartlett in 1791 and had six daughters and two sons. The latter two were Edward, b.1792 and John, b. 1795, but in the parish registers up to 1837 I found no marriages for either. It is possible that the Edward Henley, agent for Bully/Job and Company, who drowned in St. John's harbour in 1814, was John's son. I found no marriages for any of their five sisters. As none of them appear either in the 1841 or 1851 English census records it is likely they emigrated either to British North America or to the United States.

John's brother, Richard, married Joan Creed in 1792. They both lived to enjoy old age in Wolborough where they lived off Richard's earnings in the Newfoundland trade. Meanwhile they had five children, all sons. One of them, John Creed, b. 1798, became a druggist and worked in Exeter for a time. He then moved to London where he lived for a short time before settling permanently in Norwood, Surrey. He married there and had at least four children, two sons and two daughters. Sometime in the 1860's he moved his pharmaceutical practice to Lindfield, Sussex where his older son, James, lived with him as a clerk. None of James's siblings appear in any of the English census records subsequent to 1851.

John Creed's brother, William Creed, remained in Newton Abbot and made a living as a landed proprietor. In his retirement years he lived in Ringmore but continued to invest in ship owning.

Most of this family seems to have been involved in some way with the Newfoundland trade before the demise of the West Country fishery. The druggist's father, Richard, together with the latter's brother, Samuel,

and Richard Jr, had operated a mercantile
firm involved in the West Country fisheries.
From their base in Newton Abbot they traded
to Newfoundland, the Mediterranean and Devon.
They owned the 151-ton schooner, **Aurora**, with
which they freighted supplies to St. John's
and exported fish to Portugal. At least two
of the brothers, Richard Jr. and Samuel,
married in Newton Abbot but as the West
Country fisheries were winding down, only
Richard Jr. remained in the trade. I could
not find a record of his marriage but as the
baptismal records of his children identify
his wife as Margaret and, as all his children
were given Jardine as a second name, I am
concluding that her name was Margaret Jardine.
John Jardine, a draper of Newton Abbot, who
may have been Margaret's brother, formed a
partnership with Richard Jr. which permitted
the latter to continue in the Newfoundland
trade as owner of the 116-ton **Margaret**. He
was one of the last West Country men to
engage in the Newfoundland fisheries.

It is difficult for a genealogist to
reconstruct an English family tree for the
post-1837 period. That is because, generally
speaking, the parish registers have not been
archived beyond that date, for in that year
civil registration began in the United
Kingdom. Thus, while the post-1837 records
are much more informative and more easily
read than those for any other period, it is
more difficult to access them. That is
because they remain under government
management and access is granted on a fee-
paying basis. Families who wish to trace
their descent beyond 1837 should not become
discouraged because there is an avenue by
which they can retrieve marriage, birth and
death records. Orders for certificates can be
made online, by post, phone or fax and, if
you live in the UK you can obtain them in

person by visiting the Family Records Centre in London or the local register office where the event was first registered; for further details visit www.gro.gov.uk/gro/content/

Nevertheless I have been able to reconstruct some of the branches beyond 1837 by means of the various census records but I hasten to remind my readers that census records have their limitations as they cannot record the maiden name of a spouse. The post-1837 information on the Henley family trees of Newton Abbot, Dartmouth and Torquay was retrieved largely from the various census records. The reader, I hope, can therefore excuse the lack of detail in the post-1837 family trees as compared to the earlier ones.

By means of those census records I have been able to discover that Richard Henley Jr. and his wife Margaret had at least two children. They were Margaret, b. c.1827 and John Jardine, b. c. 1830. By 1851 John Jardine is studying law with the town clerk of Totnes but thereafter he disappears from the English census records. In the meantime John Jardine's uncle Samuel had married Mary Davis but had begotten only one child, a deaf-mute, who spent most of her life in an institution. It remained to Samuel Henley's two brothers, John Creed and William Creed, to preserve the family name in the Newton Abbot area. But as we have seen the family of the druggist, John Creed, had emigrated to the London area while William Creed had but two daughters. And as none of their first cousins had married in that region it meant that the extensive Henley branch originated by Edward Henley and Mary Garrett in 1757 had withered away by 1850. In fact the Henley name would have disappeared entirely from Newton Abbot/Abbotskerswell had it not been for the fact that the family of William Codner Henley had returned from Torquay to

run the cider factory. We shall continue
their story when we take up the subject of
the Torquay Henleys.

Chapter Three

The Dartmouth Henleys.

Richard Henley planted what would prove to be a rather extensive branch of the Abbotskerswell/Newton Abbot Henleys when he married Mary Roads in Dartmouth in 1668. But first we will deal with a little "twig" of the Newton Abbot Henleys that began to grow in a suburb of Dartmouth after 1762 and disappeared again by century's end.

In Chapter I we met Andrew Henley of Newton Abbot who married Mary Cole in 1721 and had two sons, Luke and John. Both of those sons took to the sea and while Luke settled in Torquay to follow his trade, John, his younger brother, gravitated to the Brixham area, closer to Dartmouth. John served on a variety of schooners such as the **Olive Branch**, the **Hawke** and the **Trial**. He had a first cousin, John, also born in Newton Abbot who was just six years younger and that gives rise to a sort of puzzle which leads to a genealogist's nightmare. For, in the event of a John Henley-marriage how can a genealogist working two hundred and fifty years later really decide who married whom? For instance a John Henley marriage took place in 1762 in a parish just a few miles from Newton Abbot and both Johns had to be considered as the likely spouse. Ordinarily, without additional evidence, one could never really be certain. But, while researching at the DRO in Exeter in 2006 I had a surprising breakthrough with the discovery of a most interesting document detailing the heart-breaking experiences of a poor man, John Henley. In December of 1757 he went before a Justice of the Peace in Chudleigh and swore out an 'Information' against some of his

former masters for non-payment of wages. He
sketched his work career for the JP, saying
'he is a sojourner there, husbandman, born in
Woolborough parish, lived with his parents
until he was about eleven years old, then he
was bound as apprentice to William Lang of
Stokeintinshead, until he was twenty-one,
then went to Newfoundland and after returning
went and served William Lang (son of former
master) in Stokeintinshead, for six months...
By the week, and then went and lived with
Henry Davis, yeoman in West Teignmouth, about
six months... by the week... then came to
Chudleigh and lived with Joseph Dolus,
butcher, about ½ year... by the week... and then
married in Chudleigh...but gained no settlement
since he worked in Stokeinteignhead'.[1] It is
clear from this evidence that the only fit
for 'Chudleigh' John is the one born to
Andrew Henley and Mary Cole in 1730.[2] We are
then left with the question of identifying
the John who married Elizabeth Mussey (Massey)
at Churston in 1762. The only John in the
entire region of South Devon who could
qualify is the first cousin of 'Chudleigh'
John mentioned above. He had been born in
1724 to John Henley and Mary Wills and as he
would have been thirty-eight we can not be
certain that he was Elizabeth's husband.
Besides, the Highweek burial records give
credence to the possibility he may have died
young and while the marriage register
described Elizabeth's husband as a "sailor"
he could well have been from some other
county in England or even from Ireland. We
will therefore leave the doubt unresolved and
for the record mention that they had four
children for whom no marriage records could

[1]Exeter, DRO: PO 12/393.
[2]Above, 105.

be found except for daughter, Susannah, who
married Francis Moxey at Brixham in 1793.[3]

Meanwhile 'Chudleigh' John married
Alice Berry and soon moved to Stoke-in-
Teignhead where he had at least one son, John,
who married Mary Martin in 1777.He went to
sea as a mariner and did well enough to
invest in a piece of land. He and Mary moved
to Bishopsteignton where they had at least
five children, four of whom seem to have
disappeared from the records. Perhaps they
died unmarried or perhaps they left Devon for
greener pastures elsewhere, either in England
or the New World. One of the family, Richard,
b.1794, married Mary Bowden from West
Teignmouth and had at least one son, Thomas.
Richard and his son Thomas were both farm
laborers who moved around the area between
Chudleigh, Bishopsteignton, Stoke-in-
Teignhead and West Teignmouth, looking for
work. It was at Chudleigh that daughter Sarah
Jane was born and at West Teignmouth that son,
Thomas was born. The census records tell us
that Thomas was born around 1830-32 and Sarah
Jane in 1841. Thomas apparently never married
and, like his father, moved around the region
working as a farm laborer. By 1881, at which
time he was past fifty years of age, he was
found in the census as a farm servant with
the family of George Bond in Stokeinteignhead.
Thus, this branch of the Henley tree, which
had begun with John Henley and Mary Martin in
1777, had died out in just over a hundred
years.

You will recall from Chapter I that we
originally encountered a dilemma regarding

---

[3]There was also a Susanna, age 29, living at St Marychurch at this time
and it could well have been she who married Francis Moxey. As this
issue can not be resolved definitively we must be content with opting
for the younger Susanna based merely on the fact that her native village
of Churston was closer to Brixham than St. Marychurch.

Richard Henley, as doubts had arisen on whether or not there were two of them at the same time, one in Abbotskerswell and one at Dartmouth. We resolved the problem in favor of one Richard who for a few years following his marriage lived in Abbotskerswell but by 1674 had settled permanently in Dartmouth. There, in addition to the two daughters he had at Abbotskerswell, Richard had two more daughters and three sons. One of the sons, William, died in infancy and a second, Richard, does not appear to have married. John, however, married twice, first to Joan Adams and, second, to Willmet Wittecer[4]. John was a rather important figure in the life of Dartmouth as witness the fact that at least by 1720 he was a churchwarden at Townstall parish and for several years in the 1730's he served in the same capacity in the other Dartmouth parish, St. Saviour. Two of his sons, John and Richard, were heavily involved in the Newfoundland fisheries.

John, b.1718, appears to have married in Brixham to Mary Bailey of Churston in 1736. That marriage is the only one in the entire region that could possibly apply to the John, son of Richard, and as both Churston and Brixham are just outside Dartmouth I am making that conclusion without claiming one hundred per cent certainty. The marriage, however, did not produce any offspring. No baptismal record survives for John's brother, Richard, and I am estimating his birth at about 1712. How do I know that he was John's brother? This is not a definitive conclusion

---

[4]There is considerable difficulty in reading this name in the Bishops Transcripts. The modern transcribers of the Devon and Cornwall Record Society have rendered the name as "Widdicar" but after very careful study of the letter formations of that period I am confident that the name is Wittecer, a precursor of the more modern name of Whittaker.

but I have looked at the entire range of possibilities in southern Devon. I have also examined the connections established by the shipping records and have concluded that there cannot be much doubt about it. He married twice, first to Jane Lannon in 1732 and secondly to Grace Preston in 1743. Both marriages gave him a total of ten children, three daughters and seven sons. Both Mary and her twin brother Richard died in infancy. I did not find any marriage for Jane, b. 1740 but her sister Joan, after having had an illegitimate son, Andrew in 1772, married William Petherbridge in 1781. In addition to the infant Richard, two other sons died in infancy while Robert does not appear to have married. Edmund, although baptized with that name, appears in the records most often as Edward. No marriage record has survived for him, yet a burial record of 1780 identifies a deceased male as "son of Edward" and one for 19 July 1789 records the burial of "Catherine daughter of Edmund and Catherine Henley". Around 1792-3 he appears to have died, for the property records show that the house and land once occupied by him as a proprietor are now being rented from "the late E Henley". [5] Following his death his widow, Catherine, with her only two children dead as well, made her living as a baker.

Edmond's name appeared frequently in the shipping records for, like his brothers and cousins, he went to sea. He served on a variety of schooners such as the **Molly**, the **Heath**, the **Honour**, the **Olive**, and the **Elizabeth**. As indicated earlier[6] there were at least four Edward Henleys involved in some way with the West Country fisheries out of Devon and St. John's by the opening of the

[5]Exeter, DRO, LTA's, Dartmouth, 1792-4.
[6]Above, 120.

19th century. From the few records that have survived it is extremely difficult, if not impossible, to sort them out correctly. But the McGrath papers at the Provincial Archives, as well as the Governor's correspondence, make several references to an Edward Henley of Dartmouth as an agent in Labrador for the Devon firm of Arthur Hunt. The first such reference is 1817 and the last one occurs in 1842. From our family tree we can tell that there are only two Edwards in Dartmouth to whom those references could apply. One is the Edward b. 1746 to Richard and Grace, and the second is his nephew, Edward Preston, b.1794 to John and Elizabeth. We must eliminate the first Edward (Edmond) because we know that he died in the mid-1790's and there can be little doubt that by 1842 Arthur Hunt's agent must be none other than Edward Preston Henley. The problem with that option was that new findings show Edward Preston as a shipwright living in Dartmouth all his life.[7] So who was the Hunt agent described as "Edward of Dartmouth"?

Complicating this problem is the fact that numerous references appear continually from 1817 onwards to Edward Henley on the Labrador coast. We must consider the possibility that if the 1746 Edward had ever been an agent for Arthur Hunt, then he was replaced sometime after 1794 with another Edward from Dartmouth. But there really is no Dartmouth Edward except the one born in 1803 who was the grand-nephew of the older Edmond (Edward) mentioned above. But even if we allow the younger Edward to become an agent at the tender age of twenty we are still left with the serious question as to

---

[7]This information comes from a variety of sources such as the Directories for the post-1800 period as well as the various censuses of England.

the identity of the Edward operating as an agent in the trans-Atlantic business of Arthur Hunt before 1823. All possibilities stretch the limits of credibility and, besides, the younger Edward appears to have remained in Devon. He engaged in mercantile business on his own account but eventually moved permanently to Plymouth. Following his move he formed a partnership with John Shepheard of that port. They carried on business as export merchants until 1862 when the partnership was dissolved. Edward married Ann Mends there and although they may have had a daughter, there are no records of any sons. So his line came to an end when he died there. I am therefore forced to conclude that the Edward Henley who was agent for Arthur Hunt did not belonged to Dartmouth at all, but was one of the Newton Abbot Henleys. It was not unusual for the Newton Abbot merchants, traders and mariners to operate out of Dartmouth and Hunt's agent fits that pattern as well.

Edward's grandfather, Richard, b. 1745, went to sea at an early age and by the time he was twenty-five was master of the **Scarborough** involved in the coasting trade between his home port and Newfoundland. In succeeding years he alternated between the positions of captain and mate on a variety of schooners plying between various English ports and Newfoundland. Eventually he became master of the **Hazard**, owned by his Wolborough cousins, Samuel and William, who operated out of St. John's as well as Devon. Richard married Agnes Dever at Berry Pomeroy in 1766[8] and had sons Richard and William. Richard jr. married Nancy Beard in 1803 and had the son Edward, of whom we wrote above.

---

[8]This is a calculated judgment on my part as there is no absolute certainty for distinguishing between the various Richards.

Richard's brother, John, b.1758, who married Elizabeth Wilcox, had five sons and six daughters but I've found marriages for only three of them. Fanny never married and spent her life as a bonnet maker in Dartmouth. Susanna married George Furneaux of Brixham in 1812 and sons, Edward Preston Henley and Thomas, married Betsy Rogers and Elizabeth Peake respectively in the same parish St. Saviour and in the same year, 1816. Both of them originated Henley branches that were still growing when we take our leave of them in the 20th century.

Edward Preston Henley made his living as a shipwright while his wife, Betsy, worked all her life as a quilter. Daughter Lydia, who never married, worked at home with her mother as a dressmaker. In addition to Lydia they had at least five other children. One of them, Edward Thomas, b.1821, formed his own small construction company and with a total of about six workers spent his life in the building trades. He married Harriet Jago and had one son, Edward J, who, when he came of age, joined his father in the business. Edward J took over the company following his father's death and married Salome Elliott of Brixham. And at the end of the century they had three children growing up in Dartmouth.

The oldest of Edward Preston Henley's sons, John Rogers, was too independent to join his father in the construction business and formed his own building company employing six people. He married Caroline Goodridge but died before his eight children were raised. His wife Caroline became a stewardess on board a Dartmouth steamer while the oldest son, John Henry, took to the sea as a mariner. Meanwhile Caroline re-married to a businessman, John Parnell, who ran a tree nursery in Totnes. Their young daughter, Blanch, lived with them as a seed-shop assistant. Daughter, Mary, married a clothing salesman, Bertram Rodway, and settled in Chiswich, Middlesex. She took her youngest sibling, Hubert, to live with them there. Thereafter I was unsuccessful in finding Hubert or any of his other siblings in subsequent census records.

Edward Preston's brother, Thomas Henley, and wife Elizabeth Peake, had a large family of twelve children, one of whom was William who married Pamela Cuming. It was their son, William Cuming Henley, b. 1860, who became the well-known ironmonger. He started out as a simple plumber but expanded along the way to found a significant plumbing firm in Dartmouth. Eventually he branched into iron work and soon became known country-wide as a famous ironmonger. From that position William Cuming dabbled in painting, natural history and antiquarianism. He wrote voluminous letters, and became a consort of famous writers and politicians in London high society. He died, unmarried, in 1919.

Although the iron-monger had acquired the security arising from his fame and fortune, it is worthy of note that it had not always been so in that family. His father, William Sr, along with eleven other siblings, had been orphaned at a very young age by the death of their father, Thomas. As was usual in the circumstances of such a large family, they were unable to resist being broken up. Joseph was apprenticed as a very young teenager to a draper in Westminster. As many of his sisters and brothers were dispersed, perhaps in like manner or sent to foster homes, it was not possible to track them down in the various census records of the later 19th century. But sons, William and John P were both raised by their uncle on their mother's side. Their uncle apprenticed young William to a tinman and it appears that this

was the base upon which William Sr. later
built up the plumbing business whose
expansion was destined to later make his son,
William Cuming Henley, well known throughout
England. Brother John P, who became an
outdoor officer with her majesty's Customs,
married Mary Elizabeth Roper and fathered at
least six children, three sons and three
daughters. Once again death stalked this
family at an early age as John P died in his
early forties. Widow, Mary, became a
laundress to support the family while young
Rosa became a boot sewer. She later became a
grocer's assistant in Kingswear where she
married John McDuerog. She took her mother to
live with them there. Her brother William
became a mason in Totnes and married Mary
Watts but she died shortly after the birth of
their only child, Louisa. The youngest in
this family, Ralph, b. 1869, became a
stonemason and moved around Devon and
Cornwall pursuing his trade. He married
Hannah Wakeham of Dartmouth and by 1901 they
were living in Devonport with four children.

I could find marriages for only one of
the iron-monger's siblings, Arthur, who
married Clara Dammerell in 1890. He became a
dairyman in Dartmouth and later opened a shop.
He entered the 20th century with one daughter,
Doris. Thus, the family line begun by the
William Cuming Henley's father was hanging by
a thread by 1901. Luckily, however, one of
the iron-monger's uncles, John P, had also
married and given rise to a substantial
family which we have detailed above. And
those families kept the Henley name alive in
the Dartmouth area, at least, for the first
few decades of the 20th century.

Chapter Four

The Torquay Henleys.

There were Henleys in the Torquay region as early as 1580 when, in that year, Otis married Emelinge Arnell at Paignton. They had at least two sons, John, b. 1581 and Otis two years later. John appears to have married twice and had at least two sons and four daughters. But following the birth of their last child in 1632 the name Henley disappears entirely from Torquay and its surrounding parishes and does not resurface again until 1741. That early branch of the Henleys in Torquay had died out.

A more permanent branch of the Henleys was planted in Torquay when Richard arrived from Abbotskerswell in 1741. Arriving in Torquay at about the same time as Richard was a Newton Abbot cousin, Luke, and, at the end of the century Richard's two nephews, William and Richard, both took up residence there as well. Luke had become a mariner working on schooners out of that port. He was born to Andrew and Mary Cole in 1723 and married Mary Furse in St. Marychurch, Torquay in 1745. They had three sons, yet none of them succeeded in perpetuating the Henley name and this branch came to an end.

The Henley name was continued in Torquay however by William, who had been born to John and Mary Rodd at Abbotskerswell in 1774. William married Susanna Bickford at St Marychurch in 1806 and settled there to raise a family of five children. William had settled in Torquay in order to follow the sea and the shipping records show him as a mariner. In fact he became captain of the schooner, **Eliza**, owned by his first cousins, William and Richard. Soon he became captain of the schooner **Mary** and by 1815 had gone into business as a merchant in Torquay. In the same year he became part owner of the **Eliza** with his cousins, William and Richard. Afterwards the schooners, **Ann** and **Susan**, were added to his operations and he became a constant trader between Newfoundland, the Mediterranean and Devon.

William Henley and Susanna had two sons and three daughters. Mary Davey married Nicholas Goodenough in Highweek while sister, Jenny, who never married, became a governess with a family in Chudleigh. Two of the three sons died as infants while the third never appears in any of the records again and must have died in infancy as well.

Meanwhile William's brother, Richard Henley, had married Mary Codner at Abbotskerswell in 1783 but his sons, Richard Codner, John Codner and William Codner all took up residence in Torquay where they engaged in the Newfoundland trade. Richard Sr, along with his cousins from Newton Abbot, acquired an interest in the 128-ton **Eliza**. A few years later it seems he and his son, Richard Codner, had become the sole owners. From the few shipping records that have survived in St. John's it appears that by 1813 there are two **Elizas** in this Henley family, one a 78-ton brig and the other a 128-ton schooner but not enough evidence is available to distinguish between the two Richards, who are the owners.

William Codner Henley became a partner in the mercantile operations of Samuel Henley, who was his first cousin, once removed. They operated in Torquay, St. John's, Carbonear and Renews. When Samuel pulled out of Renews in the post-war period their partnership there was dissolved, but William and another relative, Richard Codner, [1] founded a new company there in 1816 and carried on alone. They operated as Dealers and Chapmen until they declared bankruptcy in 1820. But they were not deterred, for after the Newfoundland trade had ceased William became an important businessman in Torquay as a cider merchant. It is quite possible that Henley withdrew his money from the Renews business to invest in the cider business in Devon.

The cider business, in which William Codner Henley had become involved, had originated in Abbotskerswell. There, in 1791, there was established the first of what would one day become a chain of cider factories throughout Devon. [2] Commercial historians, as well as everyone interested in the Henley family history, would be keenly interested in knowing who actually founded the 1791 factory. A well-known Devon historian claimed that William C. Henley of Highweek established that factory [3] but a close scrutiny of the family tree does not reveal any William C. Henley of Highweek or surrounding area, either in the baptisms or marriages, who could qualify as the subject of that reference. Unfortunately Cocks gave no reference for his claim and his source or sources cannot be verified. However if a William Henley does indeed deserve that distinction, then there are several Williams in the Newton Abbot/Abbotskerswell area who could qualify. The difficulty with following

---

[1] Keith Matthews has recorded the partnership as between William Codner Henley and Richard Codner Henley(see MHA, MNF "Richard Codner Henley"; however the *London Gazette* of 1 Aug 1820 records the partnership as between William Codner Henley and Richard Codner and I have followed the latter example.
[2] Above, Part I, Chapter V;
[3] Cocks, Dr. John Somers, **Abbotskerswell** (Abbotskerswell: John Somers Cocks, 1995), 20.

that route is that neither one of them is closely related to the Codner Henleys who clearly owned the factory by 1812. Of course one could say that the factory could well have been purchased but we have to reply: why would he sell it as he possessed a large extended family of his own. Arguments like this one, especially in genealogy, tend to go on forever so we must consider that we can never know for certain. However, I am inclined to believe that the factory had been originated by the Codners who had been involved in the cider business in Torquay and Abbotskerswell for many years antedating the Henley involvement. Indentures and wills at the Devon record Office show that in 1804 Richard Codner who owned a "cyder warehouse" in Abbotskerswell left it to his brother William in trust for their nephew John Codner Henley until he should reach the age of twenty-one at which time it would become the property of John Codner Henley.[4] Of course the identification problem is still not completely solved for we must account for the fact that the factory, shortly afterwards, became the property of John Codner Henley's brother, William Codner, and remained in his family in direct descent until its final closing in the 1930's. One could again say that John Codner may have sold it to his brother but the question would still arise:

---

[4]Exeter, DRO, Indentures, Abstracts of Title, etc,312M/TH 509-14; the same documents show that Codner devised the remainder of his lands in Abbotskerswell to John Codner Henley's brother, William Codner, who was then only thirteen years old; it is pertinent to this question to note that at that time the word "factory" was not used to denote the buildings in Devon where fruit liquor was made. Instead cider was made in buildings more like sheds etc, and sometimes called "pound houses"; on this issue see Marshall, William, **Rural Economy Of The West of England 1796, vol I** (New York: Augustus M Kelley, 1970), 224-8.

what was the reason for selling? This objection is not as valid this time as we know for certain that the business did not remain in John Codner Henley's family for very long after he turned twenty-one. It devolved in some fashion to his brother's family and remained there for the next one hundred and fifty years. Perhaps the approximately 25,000 un-indexed legal documents in the Devon record Office will some day reveal the answer.

By the early 1820's William Codner Henley of Torquay was the established owner of the Abbotskerswell cider business. By 1820 it seems that he had already left Torquay and settled next door to the factory at Abbotskerswell. Perhaps it is no coincidence that at the same time as he acquired his interest in the cider business at Abbotskerswell he declared bankruptcy in Newfoundland. One can only conclude that he withdrew his money from the Newfoundland trade to buy out his brother's interest in the cider factory.

Although William and Grace, at the time of their marriage, lived in Torquay, the demands of the cider business forced their move to Abbotskerswell where they lived at Mallands Cottage next door to the factory. Soon after their relocation to Abbotskerswell William Codner Henley established a branch office in London for the purpose of marketing his Devon cider in that capital city. To oversee this development he moved and settled in Southwark. While his wife, Grace and family, continued to live at headquarters in Abbotskerswell, William Codner lived in Southwark until his eldest son was ready to succeed him there. Around 1850 he turned over the office to his namesake and returned to Abbotskerswell where he died in 1856.

Eventually the family established a cider-making factory in Southwark as well[5] and the business prospered. In fact William Codner Henley Jr. did well enough to become a substantial shareholder in the London and County Joint Stock Banking Company, the National Provincial Bank of England and the Commercial Bank of London.

William Codner Henley Jr. married in Surrey to Grace Jenner Snell of Croydon and reared a family there, consisting of one son and two daughters. To their only son they gave the name William Codner who, in turn, succeeded to the management and ownership of the cider empire. As William Codner Jr. passed away in 1884 it meant that William Codner Henley the 3rd inherited the direction of an extensive business at the young age of twenty. He moved back to headquarters at Abbotskerswell to pursue that development. It was he who oversaw the enormous expansion of the business around the end of the 19th century and the beginning of the 20th. He also directed the consolidation of the business following World War I.[6]

William Codner Henley the 3rd married Ada Bennett and reared a family of two sons and two daughters in Abbotskerswell. Once again he maintained the well established tradition of naming a son, William Codner.

One point of interest relating to Newfoundland concerns William Codner Henley Sr. He married Grace Juliana Leaman in Torquay in 1814 and four years later had a daughter there, Mary. This same Mary became the second wife of Azariah Munden from Brigus, Newfoundland. And who was Azariah's first wife? Well, the answer is none other than Mary Henley from Torquay. The last named Mary,

---

[5]Above, 73.
[6]Above, 76-7.

three years older than her namesake, had been
born in Torquay almost next door to the other
Mary as the daughter of Samuel and Julia
Bickford and was her namesake's second cousin,
once removed. It is this, the family of
Samuel and Julia, which interests us most of
all for they were descended from the Richard
who had arrived from Abbotskerswell in 1741
and who was destined to have at least
thirteen children in Torquay and grow
branches in Newfoundland.

In addition to the cider merchant there
were eight other siblings in this family of
William Codner Henley and his wife, Grace
Juliana. Two of his sisters married
Newfoundlanders. Mary Juliana married Brigus
merchant, Azariah Munden, and reared a family
there after 1849. Maria Evens married at Bay
Roberts to the Harbour Grace merchant, Henry
T Moore and reared a family in Harbour Grace.
It is another point of amusing interest
relating to Newfoundland genealogy and
history that their son, William Codner Henley
Moore, returned to England and worked as a
clerk in the office of his uncle, William
Codner Henley, the cider merchant.

Another sibling of William Codner Jr.
was Thomas Leaman who became a surveyor and
member of the Royal Geographical Society and
practiced in Croydon, Surrey. It appears he
did well enough to study for the medical
profession and became a practicing surgeon.
He became a very wealthy man and was a
substantial shareholder in several banks such
as the London And County Joint Stock Banking
Company, the Commercial Bank of London and
the European Bank Limited. His sister,
Susannah, lived in his household and
apparently worked for her brother as a clerk.
Thomas employed two others, one as a medical
assistant and the other as a retail assistant
as well as one house servant. His sister,

Thomasina, continued to live at Newton Abbot but never married. She was well-to-do also for she became a prominent shareholder in the Merchant Banking Company of London Limited.

The first William Codner Henley, b. 1791, had three brothers, all of whom were given the second name of Codner. Two of them unfortunately died in infancy and only John Codner survived as the only sibling of the cider merchant. It appears that John Codner was the original owner of the cider factory and for some reason passed it over to his brother.[7] John Codner Henley, instead, became a tallow chandler in Torquay where he married Ann Shapley in 1808. They had two daughters and six sons. One of the sons, William Codner, followed his father in trade and became a prominent tallow chandler on Lower Union Street, Torquay. He married Mary Ann Prouse and raised a family of seven children. Eventually he established a shop at the same address and entered business as a grocer and tea dealer. He did well enough to employ a full-time house servant. His sister, Mary Codner Henley, went to Paignton and established a shop in the grocery business as well. As she was unmarried it was there that her father chose to live after he retired.

William Codner Henley and Mary Ann had four sons, two of who, Samuel and Ebenezer, never married. They worked in the grocery business with their father and took over the shop when he retired. Their sister, Mary F, never married but became a governess in Torquay. The other two brothers, Edward and William Codner Jr, married. The former married Sarah Jane Mudd and the latter, Elizabeth Bowen of Bristol. Edward worked with his brothers as a grocer's assistant while William Codner left Torquay for the

---

[7]Above, 137-9.

great city of London. There he became a cab driver. As his wife died shortly after the birth of their last child, William was forced to send his children to a foster home in Hillingdon, Middlesex. When his oldest daughter, Elizabeth, married Ernest Falkner sometime in the 1890's she took her youngest sister, Miriam, back to live with her. And we find them in the same circumstances as we take our leave of them in 1901.[8]

John Codner Henley Jr, b.1809, made his living at carpenter work but married Louisa Earle, a milliner from South Zeal. They expanded into the drapery and tea business. However in 1865 he was forced to declare bankruptcy. He died two years later. Following his death his widow declared bankruptcy as well. Louisa continued to live with her daughters who all became milliners and dressmakers. Lucy married James Taylor, a tailor from North Tawton while her sister, Eliza married James Hamer, a plumber from Exeter. While those daughters reared families in Torquay both sons left for the bright lights of London city. There they both worked in the construction industry as carpenters and builders. Edward married Mary Tomlin and at the end of the century was rearing a young family in Penge, London. His brother, William, married Susan Backaller from Thornley, Devon and by the time of the 1881 census had three sons and two daughters living in the London area. Of all the Codner Henleys who had been born in Torquay since 1783 none could be found in Torquay by 1900. As their direct Henley ancestry goes back to John of Abbotskerswell in 1728 we will take up the

---

[8]The post -1901 English census records are not yet available as they are closed to the public for one-hundred years from the date on which they were taken.

story of John's brother Richard who planted a more permanent Henley growth in Torquay.

Richard, who had been born to William Henley and Ann Churchwell at Abbotskerswell in 1716, married Elizabeth Fox of St. Marychurch, Torquay, in 1740, and settled in the latter place where they had two sons and three daughters. Sadly, Elizabeth died shortly after the birth of her last child in 1748. The child, Agnes, died in infancy that same year. Richard married a second time to Joanne Pater and had eight more children, five boys and three girls. Two sons died in infancy but the remaining five were all involved in the West Country fisheries and the Newfoundland trade.

In Torquay the oldest son, William, married Ann Lang in 1763 but they had no offspring. Richard, b. 1761, married Mary Blake in 1801 at Totnes and had two daughters, Maria and Mary, born in 1801 and 1806 respectively. Richard's brother John married Mary Shapley in Torquay in 1794. He was the first in this large family to be converted to Methodism and at a very early age became a local preacher in St Marychurch. [9] Shortly after his marriage to Mary in 1794, however, he went to an early death.

John's brother, Edward, who married Elizabeth Shapley at St. Marychurch in 1796 had much better luck than John. It is quite possible that the Shapleys played a large part in bringing this family of Henleys to Methodism for not only were brothers Edward and John married to Shapleys but their first cousin, once removed, John Codner Henley, who was also a committed Wesleyan, married a Shapley as well. Nevertheless Rev William

[9]Henley, Rev William, "Memoir of Mr. Edward Henley" *Wesleyan Methodist Magazine for 1848:* Fourth Series, vol IV-Part II (London: John Mason, c.1849).

Henley reports that his grandparents had both been Nonconformists although they attended the parish church.[10]

Edward became a very prominent farmer in the Torquay region eventually acquiring a substantial quantity of land. He made his first land acquisition in the area when he purchased his first farm in Tormoham in 1799 from Sir Laurence Palk, the largest landowner in the Torquay region. He continually added to his holdings so that by 1825 he was proprietor of eight estates. They were known by the names of Daisy Park, Dunstones, Orchards, Lanes, part of Jeffrey's, Three Corners, Coombpafford and Middlepark.

Edward reared beef cattle and butchered them for the local market. However it was his service to Wesleyan Methodism that established his reputation in Torquay. He had been involved in the Newfoundland fisheries and was bent on a seafaring life but at the age of twenty was converted to Methodism by his older brother, John. When the latter sadly suffered an early death Edward took his place as the local preacher and over the next fifty years distinguished himself and his family by his devotion to the cause of Methodism in Torquay.[11]

At the time of his conversion Edward had been engaged to be married but he considered his fiancée unsuitable because she was not of like mind in religion. He, therefore, broke off the relationship. He met and married another convert, Elizabeth Shapley, and together they moved to Torquay to establish Methodism there. They opened their residence for religious service and became the first to preach Methodism in Torquay. The landlord later ejected them but

---

[10]Ibid.
[11]Ibid.

they soon acquired a place of their own where they continued the services. It soon became too small to accommodate their adherents and Edward therefore built his own Methodist chapel which remained his private property throughout his lifetime. It was the first such chapel in Torquay and when he died he willed the chapel to his son, Edward.

Edward's success was not however achieved without trial, for numerous obstacles were placed in his path. He encountered "...showers of stones, brickbats, and other offensive missiles" but none deterred him. "His strict integrity, his unimpeachable veracity, his uniformly blameless life, his kindness to all, his patience under inflicted wrongs, and his resignation in affliction, secured him the respect both of all denominations of Christians, and of all ranks in society".[12]

Elizabeth (Shapley) Henley was probably just as responsible as her husband, Edward, for planting Methodism in Torquay. She had been converted to Methodism at about the same time as Edward Henley and her well-known son, the Wesleyan Minister, William, described her in later years as a "saint" of a woman. In addition to Edward Jr., she and Edward Sr. had at least nine other children.[13] One of them was the famous Wesleyan Minister, William, mentioned above. He served in various charges around the Westcountry before he retired to Torquay. Edward Jr also became a Wesleyan Methodist minister. He inherited the farm from his father and carried on the rearing and butchering of beef cattle. In addition to his own family he housed his

---

[12]Ibid.

[13]In the "Memoir..." Rev William reports that his parents had eleven children but I was unable to find more than ten in the records; perhaps one died in infancy before the baptismal service could be performed.

niece, two butcher's servants, and a lodger who worked for him as a carpenter. His brother, Robert, b. 1814, became a master builder and formed his own construction company. By the 1850's he was employing twelve men. He had an only son, Frank, who gained fame for his courage and conviction in the face of a potentially fatal illness at a very young age. While still in his early twenties Frank contracted an inoperable lung disease and was advised by his doctor to consider traveling to the Antipodes in hopes that it might restore him to health. So he set off on a tour of Australia and New Zealand while along the way, and up to the very moment of death, he wrote inspirational letters to his family and friends. [14] Those letters show what an exceptional human being Frank Henley had become but his qualities were best summed up by Rev P. Hawkes at a memorial service in Torquay on Feb 28, 1886. Hawkes declared that Frank's life revealed a man possessed "...of a clear intellect, of faith in God, of love for man, of intelligent and deep thankfulness for the past, and of a never-wavering trustfulness and unshadowed

---

[14]Henley, Frank, **Bright Memories: Being Reminiscences Of Frank Henley Containing An Account Of His Visits To Australia And New Zealand** (Torquay: W H Goss "Albion" Printing Works, 1887); I first learned of this book on searching the Burnet-Morris index at the Westcountry Studies Library in Exeter, Devon in the spring of 2006. Burnett-Morris had labeled it as a "rare" book and I subsequently discovered that no Library in Devon possessed a copy. My search of libraries and old booksellers in England produced no results but after a year of searching the world by means of the internet I was rewarded with the discovery that the Public Library in Dallas, Texas possessed a copy. Incredibly, they proved so co-operative that they provided me with a copy free of charge. For assistance in locating this book I want to thank www.genuki.org.uk/devon and Daniel Morgan of Vienna, Virginia, USA.

hope for the future...." [15] But above all his sense of humour and his concern for his fellow man stood out above everything else. He continually read holy books but on his death bed was so weak that he could not hold a book about St. Paul. He was not too weak though to write his sister and tell her that he had to give up reading St. Paul because the reading "... was too heavy...". His concern for his fellow man went so far that on the night before his death he asked for a drink of water but only drank a little from a proffered glass, fearing that if he drank any more there would not be enough left for the rest of the family. A few hours later at Sandhurst, Victoria, in the early morning of January 4, 1886 he passed away. He was only twenty seven.

I have not been able to find any marriages for the daughters of Edward Henley and Elizabeth Shapley in the pre-1837 period. It is possible however that the youngest, Anna, who became a governess, married in the period following 1837. At least four of the sons were married though, viz: the two ministers, William and Edward as well as Robert and John. As Frank, above, had been Robert's only son this branch died out when Frank's sisters either married or died. Rev William's branch suffered the same fate as he had an only child, Rosa Mary. He had served charges in Cornwall and Somerset as well as in Devon. His wife belonged to Barnstaple but it was in Somerset that Rosa was born.

Rev. Edward married Elizabeth Rendle and had an only son, Richard, who peculiarly left a comfortable situation with a promising future, in Devon, to roam the world, ending up in Australia. He was married in Melbourne in 1856 and had a son Richard the following

---

[15] Ibid, 8.

year. Just a few months after his son was born Richard died. When Richard Jr. grew up he must have been seized with the desire to find out more about the father he never knew because he found his way back to England and Devon. He married Mary Haydon of London and finally settled right in Torquay where his father had been born. He raised a family there, one of whom was Albert George, who established a business in boot and shoemaking in Torquay. But Albert enlisted during World War I and was killed in action in 1918. He left a widow, Ethel Perring, whom he had married in 1912 and a three year old daughter, Winnifred. Also left in Torquay to mourn his death were sister, Bessie (William Wilson) and a brother, William Frederick, married there to Beatrice Grant Lee.

Samuel, b. 1763, was another brother of Edward, the cattleman and famous clergyman. Samuel was the man who planted his roots in Newfoundland and to those we shall now turn. But before we leave the Torquay Henleys we must record the presence of another Henley family in Torquay, by 1871, who did not belong to our south Devon Henleys at all. John Henley belonged to a family of agricultural laborers from Broadclyst and sometime in the 1840's migrated to Torquay looking for work. He and his wife Ann reared a large family of nine children, the youngest of whom, Charles, was born around 1869. The 1871 census also shows a laborer, Thomas Richard Henle (with no 'y') from Moretonhampstead, rearing a family in Torquay with wife Ann who was a railway porter. They should not be confused with the Henleys of whom we have been writing above.

Chapter Five

The Newfoundland Henleys.

Samuel, son of Richard Henley and
Joanne Pater, was born in Torquay in 1763,
the same year that his step-brother, William,
was married. It is no surprise to learn that
Samuel took to the sea, having been brought
up in that seaport town with many relatives
already involved in the international trade
and fisheries. He first appeared as a seaman
but soon went into business on his own
account, trading out of Torquay. He formed a
partnership with William Codner Henley, the
son of his first cousin, Richard, and
established a mercantile base in Torquay from
where they branched out to Carbonear, St.
John's and Renews. They owned at least two
schooners, the **Juno** and the **Hiram** which they
used to supply their operations in
Newfoundland and export their fish to the
Mediterranean. In St. John's they carried on
a general dealership selling wine and other
goods as well as provisions for the fishery.
Samuel wed Julia Bickford in 1802 at
Wolborough[1], Newton Abbot, and had at least
eight children. As Samuel owned several
schooners and was involved in the West
Country fisheries from ports in Devon and
Newfoundland, the family was quite mobile.
While he was married at Wolborough, Newton
Abbot, the baptismal records show that some
of their children were baptized in Torquay
but at least one, Eliza, was baptized in
Newton Abbot. No complete record of their
children's births or baptisms exists anywhere
and only five have been discovered to date:

---

[1]In the early records it frequently appears as "Wolboro" but its modern
official name is "Wolborough".

William, born 1802, Julia, bap. 1804, Samuel,
bap. 1807 and Mary Grace, bap.1815, all
baptized at St. Marychurch, Torquay;
Elizabeth was baptized at Highweek, Newton
Abbot in 1810 but there are no birth or
baptismal records for James J, Philip or Mary.
From marriage records and death notices, plus
the known birth dates of several of James J's
siblings, I am estimating his birth at 1805.
Due to the fact that he was referred to as "a
native of Carbonear", there is a strong
likelihood that he was born there. As for
Philip, we have only his marriage record for
1834 and, given the birth dates of his
siblings, we can therefore estimate his birth
at 1809. When Mary Grace (Munden) died in
1848 the local newspapers referred to her as
"the third daughter" of Mr. Samuel Henley and
I am therefore calculating the birth of her
sister Mary to be around 1817. That guess is
based on the fact that records show both
Eliza and Julia Bickford to have been older
than Mary Grace. Oral traditions in the
Henley family have maintained that there was
a John in this family as well, who married a
Fry. That has received some credence by
discovery of a marriage record in St. John's
of a John Hanley who was married in the
Church of England in 1830. Due to the fact
that 19th century records often used the names
Hanley and Henley interchangeably one is
tempted to consider John's marriage as
confirming the oral traditions. However, the
officiating clergyman records John as a
merchant "of London" which should rule him
out as belonging to our Henley family.
Additional evidence is provided by the fact
that he signed his own name to the marriage
document as "John Hanley".

It is quite possible, though, that
several of Samuel's children, in addition to
James J, were born in Newfoundland. The

baptisms of Julia and Mary Grace took place
in December at St. Marychurch and neither
their birth dates nor places of birth were
entered. The late fall baptismal dates would
be consistent with their having been born in
Newfoundland and thus baptized following the
journey home in the fall.

The end of the Napoleonic Wars
witnessed serious downturns in the economy of
Britain and her colonies and within a
generation the West Country fisheries came to
a complete close. The post-1815 period saw
Samuel's business suffer serious retrenchment.
In that period Samuel withdrew from the
partnership at Renews and the firm of Henley
and Codner was dissolved. He appears to have
withdrawn from Carbonear as well. While
Samuel may have lived at Carbonear and
Torquay intermittently, it seems that
sometime around 1815 he settled permanently
in Newfoundland.

Samuel's business operations were
confined entirely to St John's from that time
until his death there in 1831. Samuel's sons,
Philip and James J, remained in Carbonear
where they carried on a fishery business on
their own account, although on a much smaller
scale. While they continued as ship owners,
fishers and sealers it does not appear that
they engaged in the supplying business.
Philip married Ellen James in Carbonear but
the records show no children for this couple.
But marriage records for 1859 at Carbonear
reveal a marriage of Phillip Henley to Mary
White and it might be reasonable to conclude
that this was Phillip Jr. There can be no
certainty on this issue however because it
could well have been a second marriage for
Phillip Sr. No children appear in the records
for Phillip and Mary.

James J., on the other hand, had a
large family but they all eventually deserted

Carbonear and settled in St. John's. Although no record has surfaced to reveal when James closed out the Carbonear business I have been able to determine that he was still living there in 1855. It seems that he retired to St. John's where he died in 1879.

Samuel's daughter, Mary, whom I have estimated was born around 1817, may have been born in Carbonear. She married James Crawford. Julia, b.1804, married in St. John's, in 1831 to Capt. William Hart of Kingskerswell, Devon but she died at an early age in 1844. William Hart, according to the South African branch of this family, then married her sister, Eliza. This second marriage gave birth to a daughter who married a MacMuldrow from Liverpool and their son, W. G. P. MacMuldrow of South Africa, compiled a family tree in 1935 and sent a copy to W. A. Munn of St. John's. In that compilation he referred to our Samuel Henley as "Samuel Codner Henley of Abbotskerswell" But Mr. MacMuldrow made some obvious errors in his family tree for he identified William Codner Henley as Samuel's son whereas we know for certain that the William born to Samuel and Julia was really William Bickford Henley and that William Codner Henley belonged to a different branch of the Devon Henleys entirely.[2]

The oldest son, William Bickford, followed his father in the sea-going trades. He operated out of Carbonear and Harbour Grace until 1832, at which time he moved to Nova Scotia in charge of the brigantine **Molly Moore**. He first settled at River Phillip, Nova Scotia, but later moved to Kolbec where he raised a large family. His brother, Samuel Jr, became a medical doctor and served at Ferryland, Newfoundland. There, in 1830, he lost his life in a shooting accident. He was

---

[2]Above, Part II, Chapter IV.

not quite twenty-four years of age. Their
sister, Mary Grace, married Azariah Munden, a
master mariner, planter and ship-owner of
Brigus, and had four children before dying at
the early age of thirty-three in 1848. She is
buried in Brigus and has a tombstone which
still stands today. We have already seen that
their brother, Phillip, did not father a
permanent Henley branch and thus the Henley
line in Newfoundland would have come to an
end had it not been for James J.

James J. married in the Roman Catholic
Church at Harbour Grace in 1832 to Julia
McCarthy. Heretofore this Henley family had
been Methodists and had played an extremely
valuable role in developing Methodism in
Torquay.[3] James's marriage to Julia, however,
inaugurated a Roman Catholic branch to this
family. The large family of six daughters and
three sons which they raised in Carbonear
became the base of a new, distinct,
Newfoundland, Roman Catholic tree. The oldest
surviving daughter, Mary, married Capt. James
Stafford in St. John's. Eliza died unmarried
at the age of twenty-five and no marriage
records exist for sisters, Teresa, b.1833,
Ann, b.1836 and Teresa, b.1842. Sister Ellen
settled in St. John's where she married John
Kinsella of the Post Office. John Henley
never married while his brother Bernard
settled in St. John's and married Mary Ann
Byrne in 1882. They had several children, but
all died in infancy.

James J's son, Charles, born in
Carbonear in 1847, perpetuated the Henley
line by marrying Catherine Fitzpatrick in St.
John's in 1869. They had four children before
he succumbed to a sudden death in 1882. He
was visiting the United States on business at
the time of his death and consequently was

---

[3] Above, Part II, Chapter IV.

buried in Gloucester, Massachusetts. His daughter, Mary, married Edward Cahill who had a hardware business on Water Street. Julia Ann married Vincent Gosse, a St. John's tailor. James, who was a fireman in St. John's, married Margaret Evans.

The most prominent of Charles's children was John J, who established the well-known mattress factory whose history we chronicled in Part I, chapter VI. John J was a tall, imposing figure perhaps not unlike his son, Ted, who, when I worked for him at Pan American Airways in Gander in the 1950's, resembled in stature the Heavyweight boxing champion of the world. John J's heart was big too as every spring he would send his bedspring repair and mattress crews to St. Bon's Boarding school, Littledale Boarding School, Belvedere Orphanage and Mt. Cashel. All work and repairs were completed at his own expense. When, in the early nineteen-twenties, a fire at Mt. Cashel forced all orphans and personnel on the streets Henley provided over one-hundred mattresses at his own expense so they all could be housed at St. Bon's until repairs made the orphanage livable again.

He was famed as a singer and in his day was the lead singer in the Basilica choir. John J and a few of his friends created the famous Shanahan band of the St. John's music circuit. They performed a variety of concerts to raise money for their favorite charities. There is a strong oral tradition that it was John J for whom Daniel Carroll wrote the famous Newfoundland ballad, *The Star of Logy Bay.*

John J. married twice, first to Isabelle Armstrong and after her death to Catherine Ellen Brennan. By his first wife John J. had eight children, two girls and six boys. Mary, the eldest, became a Mercy Nun and taught school at various places throughout the province. At North River she became superior of the convent and principal of All Hallows High School. In the nineteen sixties she served four years as principal of St. Pius X School in the capital and eventually became bursar of the Mercy Order. Her only sister, Isabelle, graduated from the Grace Maternity Hospital in 1929-30 with a Registered Nurse designation. In 1933-34 the Commission of Government appointed her as District Nurse in Rencontre West where she resided until 1938. She then returned to the Grace Hospital as Supervisor of the Grace Maternity Ward. She later married an American serviceman, Peter Downey, from the Fort Pepperell base and moved to the United States.

Leo had taken over as manager of the manufacturing business in the mid-nineteen-thirties. He was quite athletic but health problems weakened him considerably. While convalescing from an appendix operation Leo succumbed to tuberculosis in 1936. Another son, Thomas, a candidate for the jubilee scholarship, died in April, 1929 at the age of seventeen. His brother, John, a promising young singer, died at the age of twenty-nine. He fell through the ice at a skating party on Burton's Pond, caught a series of colds and never recovered. He succumbed two years afterwards from influenza, pneumonia and tuberculosis.

Charles began work with a commercial cable company, left it to become a forestry surveyor, and then established his own business as a commission agent. During the war he closed it out to work as a financial supervisor with the American army at Fort Pepperell. Jim worked in the department of education, with the Council of Higher Education but died in his twenties from tuberculosis. Frank, another of the Henleys highly regarded for his singing talents, worked at the Canadian Consul office where he was encouraged to pursue a university career. He thus attended Queen's University in Kingston, ON and graduated with a commerce degree. He married a Newfoundland girl, Clare Noseworthy, and they lived and raised a family in London, Ontario.

John J's second marriage to Catherine Brennan produced five children, two girls and three boys. Catherine, who managed the firm's accounts for the Mattress factory married Dick Harris. Dick was a storekeeper who owned and operated Dick's Jewellery on Water St in St. John's. It was their son, John James (Jack) who was elected to the House of Commons as a New Democratic Party representative for St. John's East in 1987. In 1990 Jack was elected to the Provincial House of Assembly for St. John's East and in 1992 was elected leader of the Newfoundland and Labrador New Democratic Party. He served his St. John's district as MHA and continued to lead the NDP until his retirement from active politics in 2006. It was Jack's brother, Richard (Rick), who founded Eastern Audio, renowned today in the communications field in Newfoundland.

Catherine's sister, Mary, the youngest in the family attended Mount St. Vincent University in Nova Scotia and became a teacher of music. She joined the Sisters of Charity where she served for over twenty years before leaving to teach in British Columbia. At the age of seventy-two she completed a Ph. D in English from the University of British Columbia. She is presently living in retirement in Vancouver.

Catherine's brother, Patrick, took over the management of the Mattress factory following the death of his father. [4] In his

---

[4] Above, 88.

youth Pat was highly regarded as an athlete and was an excellent footballer. He married Mary Battcock and had one son, Stephen.

Ted attended Memorial University and was a good athlete, singer and amateur actor. In 1937 he left Newfoundland to join the Royal Flying Corps in England, later transferring to the Royal Air Force. In the following year he became a pilot officer and was sent to Canada where RAF pilots were trained for war duties. He soon was promoted to acting wing commander. He later served in the Caribbean Command from the Bahamas. From there he proceeded to Iceland where he served in the Coastal Command and was mentioned in despatches. Afterwards he was transferred to England and was assigned reconnaissance duties over Europe. Following the war he joined Pan American Airlines in Gander as a dispatcher and later became manager. He retired in the 1960's from that position to become Director of Tourism with the Provincial Government in St. John's. He left to serve briefly as St John's city manager before permanently retiring to live in the capital.

Alec, the twelfth of John J's thirteen children, attended St. Bonaventure's College in St. John's and graduated in 1941. He immediately began work as a land surveyor with the Canadian Department of Transport and became part of the team that surveyed the land that one day would become Torbay Airport. But in 1944 he left that field of endeavour to become an insurance underwriter. Later he studied by correspondence at the University of Toronto and in 1953 received his Chartered Life Underwriter's Degree, C.L.U. The following year, at the age of thirty-two, he founded the company which today still bears his name. Known as **Alec G Henley & Associates**, as well as **The Alec G Henley Group**, the firm has become a company leader in the independent life and disability insurance field.

Under Alec's guidance, his insurance firm has grown and developed into a full service Independent Employee Benefit and Financial Advisory firm which specializes in providing advice on Group Employee Benefits, Group Pensions, Group Retirement and Executive Compensation Consulting Services. In addition the company's Financial Advisory Practice specializes in the areas of Personal Financial Planning, Estate Planning, Retirement Planning, Business Succession Planning and Wealth Management. The company does business throughout Newfoundland And Labrador and Maritime Canada, as well as in the international market.

Having achieved great success in founding and operating his own firm Alec has been involved in the Newfoundland business community in numerous other capacities as follows: Board Chair & President, Carpasia Investments Inc; Board Chair & President, Carpasia Properties Limited; Director and Partner, Maritime Mortgage Co; Director and Partner, Forest Manor Real Estate; Partner, Torbay Estates; Founding Chairman and Chief Executive Officer of Avalon Cablevision Limited, 1975-1979; (From the start of the company until he resigned as Board Chair the bulk of the cable network system in the greater St Johns area had been constructed and the company had penetrated sixty-eight percent of the market); Executive Committee Member, Newfoundland Cablevision Consortium; Director of Canadian Cable Television Association (CCTA), 1976-79; founding President of Sportscraft, a Water Street sports equipment store; CEO of Dominion Distributors Ltd; Vice-President, B.I.L. Limited; Founding Member of the Newfoundland

Life Underwriter's Association, 1949; Vice-President of the Newfoundland Life Underwriter's Association, 1949; President of the Newfoundland Life Underwriter's Association, 1950 and Faculty Member, Atlantic Life Insurance School.

From his early days Mr. Henley has been extensively involved in community and church affairs. He loved sports and took part in curling, rowing and golf. Hi involvement in rowing earned him an Honorary Life Membership in the Royal St. John's Regatta Committee in 1988. In 1997 he was inducted into the Regatta Hall of Fame. As a volunteer Alec has been involved in politics at the municipal, provincial and federal levels and served as a Municipal Councillor in St. Johns from 1957-65. His contributions to his church were recognized by Pope John Paul II in 1985 when he was made Knight of the Order of St. Gregory.

Alec Henley married Catherine Tobin in 1948 and they are very proud of the family they raised together. They commenced the post-secondary education of their four children by sending each in turn to Neuchatel, Switzerland. There they graduated from Neuchatel Junior College with an equivalent of Ontario grade thirteen.

Their only daughter, Janet, holds a Bachelor of Arts degree in Mathematics from Memorial University and a law degree from the University of Toronto. She practiced law in St. John's with the firm, Stirling, Ryan et al. and its successor, Stewart McKelvey Stirling Scales, from 1980 to 2007. In 2001 she was appointed Queen's Counsel. During the province's Denominational Education debate in the 1990's Janet was a leader in the advocacy for Catholic education and served on the Catholic Education Committee, 1997-8 and the Inter-Denominational Committee, 1997-8.

Following an amendment to the Canadian constitution in 1998 she became a founding member of the new St. Bonaventure's College, an independent Catholic school in the Jesuit tradition. Since that date she has served as Vice-Chair of the Board of Directors as well as Chair of fundraising.

Alec's son, John J, graduated from Memorial University in 1981 with a Bachelor of Arts degree in Mechanical Engineering. Following this he completed two Master's degrees from the Massachusetts Institute of Technology, one in Ocean Engineering and the other in Ocean Systems Management. He has worked for a number of Canadian oil companies, and held senior positions with Hibernia Management and Development and Newfoundland Transshipment Limited. He was recently appointed to the Board of Directors of Marine Atlantic.

Alec's youngest son, Christopher, graduated from Memorial University in 1980 with a Bachelor's degree in Mathematics following which he completed a Master's Degree in Business Administration at Dalhousie University in Halifax. He worked extensively in the oil and gas field at Calgary and Toronto, and afterwards developed a comprehensive portfolio in the field of investment dealing. In 1995 he became a Director and Senior Vice-President of Canaccord Capital Corporation and headed that firm's Technology and Communications Practice. At the same time he founded Henley Capital Corporation, a limited market dealer specializing in advising and financing both public and private companies in the technology and emerging growth sectors. At the time of writing he is President and CEO of that firm which operates from offices in Toronto.

Alec's oldest son, Brian A, graduated from Memorial University in 1979 with a Bachelor of Commerce Degree and then joined his father's firm. He afterwards obtained designations as Chartered Life Underwriter, Chartered Financial Consultant and Certified Financial Planner. He has served, and continues to serve, as member and director of numerous boards and committees in the financial field. These include founding member of the Newfoundland and Labrador Advisory Board of Certified Employee Benefit Specialists, and founding Chair of the Basilica Foundation Inc. In 2005 he became president and Chief Executive Officer of Alec G Henley & Associates Ltd. and in 2008 was appointed a member of the Board of Directors of the Bank of Canada.

Having designated his son, Brian A Henley, as CEO of Alec G Henley & Associates in 2005, one would have expected Alec to retire from the firm he founded in 1954. But after more than fifty years of involvement, and at the age of eighty five, you will still find him regularly at his desk in his downtown, St. John's office. In addition Alec still finds time and energy to remain active in community and church affairs.

Chapter Six: Postscript.

The attempt to construct the Henley family tree is beset with the usual problems associated with the study of genealogy. One such example is the presence of so many individuals in a particular family tree being given the same personal name. The difficulty is compounded by the fact that some of them were born within a few years of one another. If we look at the marriage of Richard Henley and Mary Codner in 1783 we are faced with just such a dilemma. The fact that there was a Richard Henley born in Torquay in 1761 and another one born at Abbotskerswell around 1762 compounds the identification question. I have resolved this particular problem by opting for the Abbotskerswell Richard because the marriage took place at Abbotskerswell and because the only surviving baptismal record for an offspring, Richard Codner Henley, 1784, shows Abbotskerswell as the place of christening.

Complicating that decision is the existence of marriage records in Torquay of John Codner Henley and William Codner Henley. As both these men bear the Codner name we must assume they were also the sons of Richard Henley and Mary Codner, even though the baptismal records necessary to confirm their identification are missing. Mary Codner's marriage is the first Codner marriage amongst the Henleys and there would be no reason to insert that Codner name except in the children of Richard and Mary above.

Nevertheless, the problem is further confused by the fact that William MacMuldrow, a Henley descendant in South Africa, referred, in his compilation of a family tree in 1935, to the Samuel, born 1763, as Samuel **Codner**

Henley.[1] If that were true then we would have
to reconsider the logic of using Codner as a
middle name and rethink our decision
regarding the marriage of Richard Henley and
Mary Codner. But why would Samuel have the
middle name of Codner? It did not appear in
his baptismal record, nor on the baptismal
records for any of his brothers and sisters.
Normally one would defer to a family member
such as the South African descendant,
MacMuldrow, but in this case he has made at
least one clear mistake. He noted that Samuel
was a native of Abbotskerswell whereas I have
proven, with the assistance of records in
Devon, that Samuel belonged to Torquay.[2]
Therefore, doubt must be cast on his claim
that Samuel had the middle name of Codner as
well as on his remaining claims.

In addition to the problems outlined
above there are the problems with regards to
lack of records as well as the incompleteness
of those which exist[3]. Those lead, inevitably,
to a number of unresolved questions. For
example in the Highweek baptismal records for
1798 there is a christening on Jan 1 of John,
son of John Henley and Elizabeth Shapley.
But there is no marriage in those records for
John and Elizabeth and none could be found in
the adjacent parishes. So who is this John
Henley? Interestingly, just a few miles to
the south at Torquay we find John Henley
marrying **Mary** Shapley in 1794, and in 1796,
in the same parish, Edward marries **Elizabeth**
Shapley. In the Torquay records there are no
baptisms for any children of John and Mary,
so did they move to Highweek where some
official made a mistake in his wife's name? I
tend to believe it was the latter as both

[1]Above, 153.
[2]Exeter, DRO, 312M/TH510: Indenture, 10 Mar 1818.
[3]Above, 95-7.

brothers, John and Edward, were married to Shapleys.

I would like to focus on a particular problem which becomes one of enormous significance for the Henley genealogy. That issue is the presence in St. John's in the 18th century of Henleys who cannot be integrated into our Henley family tree. The Church of England parish registers in St. John's identify a Roger Henley married to Mary Butler in 1759. No other information is given and one is left to wonder if there was a Henley family line in St. John's at that time. Again the burial records of that church witness to a death of Mary Henley in 1760. Who was this Mary? Was she Roger's infant daughter or was she Roger's wife? And if the latter, did Roger marry again? The problem is compounded by the appearance in the Governor's records of a John Henley who is a householder in St. John's as well as a Samuel Webber Henley, a ship owner who belonged to St. John's. Then in 1780 and 1781 Roger and Bartholomew Henley appeared as householders in St. John's. In the four hundred and fifty years of Henley genealogy which has been collected to date the names of Bartholomew and Webber never appear amongst the Henleys while the name of Roger Henley appears only once, in Exeter in 1635. It leads one to entertain the idea that there might be Henleys from other counties besides Devon not only engaged in the Newfoundland trade but living and rearing families in St. John's at the end of the eighteenth century. That has been confirmed by several records showing the mercantile involvement of several Henleys from London. One should not therefore be concerned with multiple appearances of Henley names in St. John's around 1800 that can not be integrated into Alec Henley's family tree.

Chapter Seven (1 of 42)

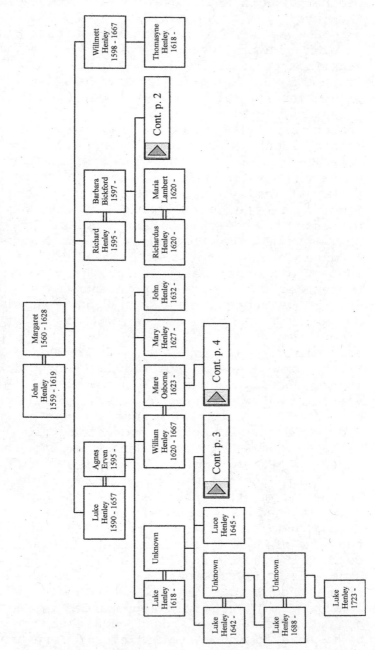

Chapter Seven (2 of 42)

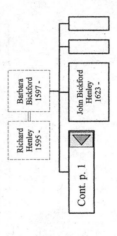

Chapter Seven (3 of 42)

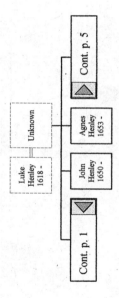

Chapter Seven (4 of 42)

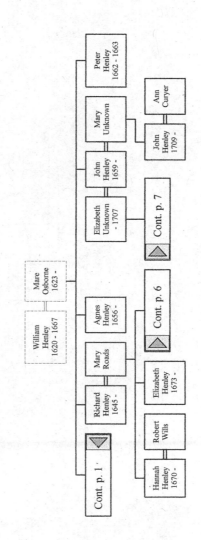

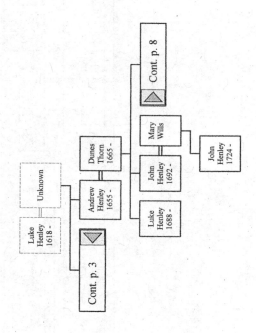

Luke
Henley
1618 -

Unknown

Andrew
Henley
1655 -

Dunes
Thorn
1665 -

Cont. p. 3

Luke
Henley
1688 -

John
Henley
1692 -

Mary
Wills

Cont. p. 8

John
Henley
1724 -

Chapter Seven (6 of 42)

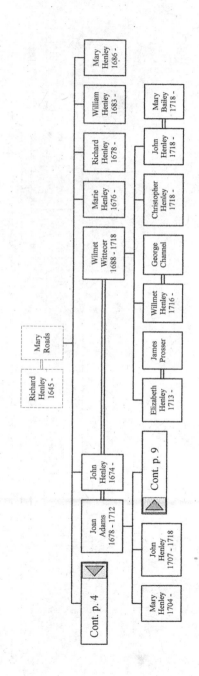

Chapter Seven (7 of 42)

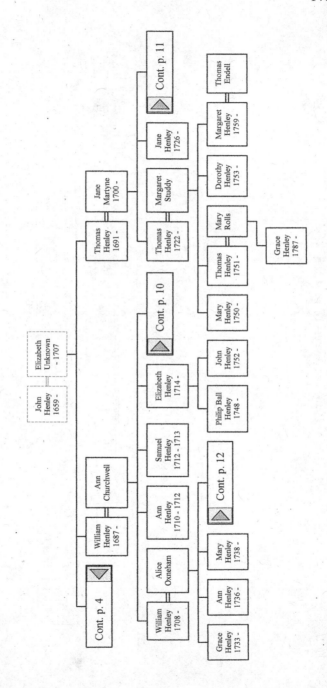

Chapter Seven (8 of 42)

```
                    Andrew
                    Henley
                    1655 -
                       |
                    Dunes
                    Thorn
                    1665 -
```

Andrew Henley 1694 - — Mary Cole 1700 -

Elizabeth Henley 1697 -

Edward Henley 1699 -

Cont. p. 5 ▽

Luke Henley 1723 - — Mary Furse 1725 -

John Henley 1730 - — Allice Berry

Luke Henley 1746 - 1746

Ann Henley 1751 -

Sarah Henley 1755 - 1757

Luke Henley 1759 -

Jane Henley 1760 -

William Henley 1764 -

John Henley 1758 - — Mary Martin

William Henley 1786 -

Mary Henley 1787 -

Elizabeth Henley 1789 - — William Baker

Thomas Henley 1792 -

Richard Henley 1794 - — Mary Bowden

Thomas Henley 1832 -

Sarah Jane Henley 1841 -

Chapter Seven (9 of 42)

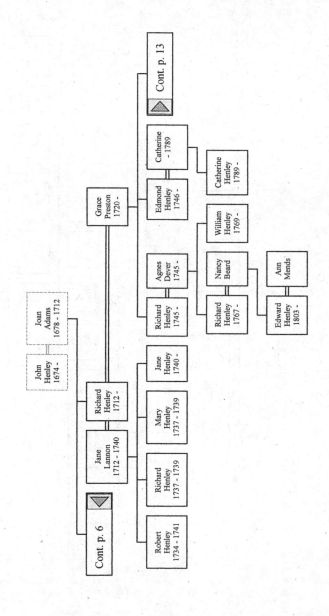

Cont. p. 13

Cont. p. 6

Chapter Seven (10 of 42)

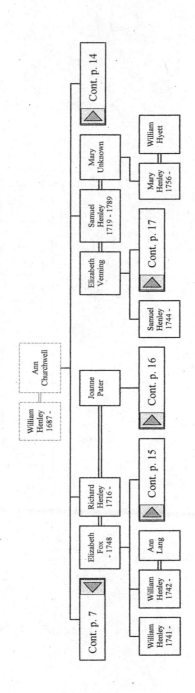

Chapter Seven (11 of 42)

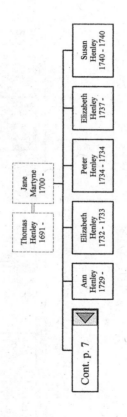

Cont. p. 7

Chapter Seven (12 of 42)

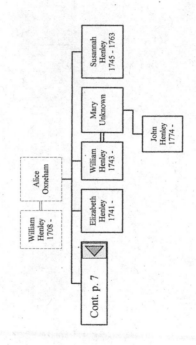

Chapter Seven (13 of 42)

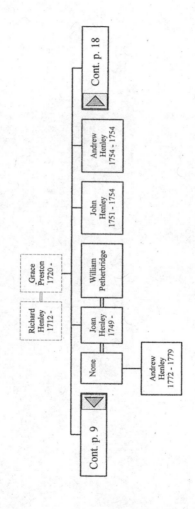

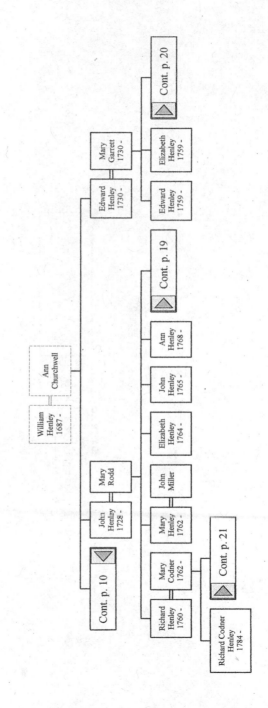

Chapter Seven (15 of 42)

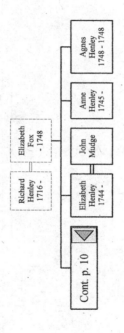

Richard
Henley
1716 -

Elizabeth
Fox
- 1748

Elizabeth
Henley
1744 -

John
Mudge

Anne
Henley
1745 -

Agnes
Henley
1748 - 1748

Cont. p. 10

Chapter Seven (16 of 42)

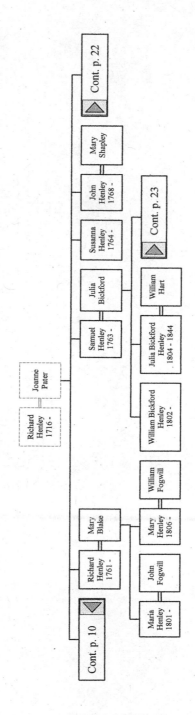

Cont. p. 22

Cont. p. 23

Cont. p. 10

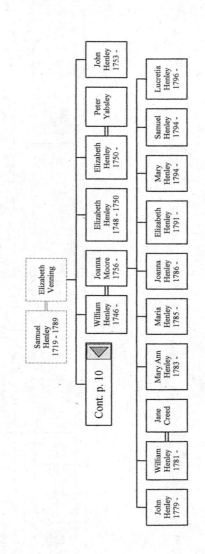

Cont. p. 10

Chapter Seven (18 of 42)

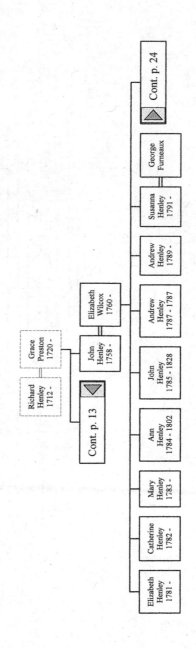

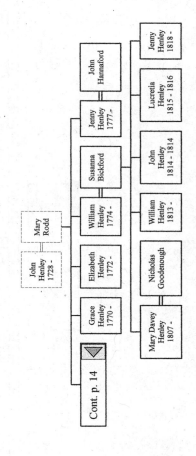

Chapter Seven (20 of 42)

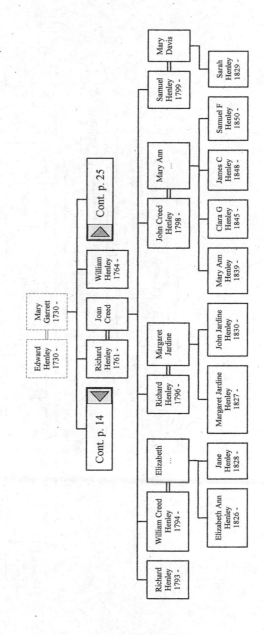

Chapter Seven (21 of 42)

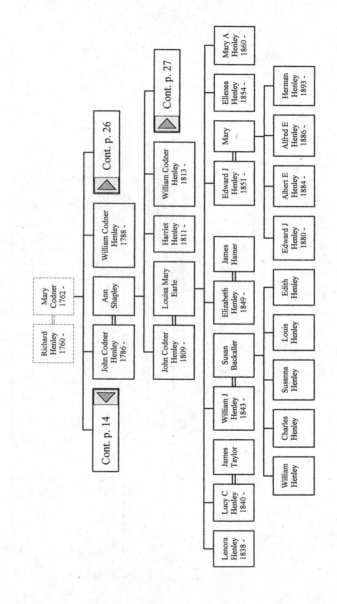

Chapter Seven (22 of 42)

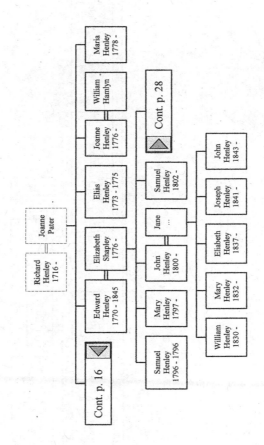

Cont. p. 16

Cont. p. 28

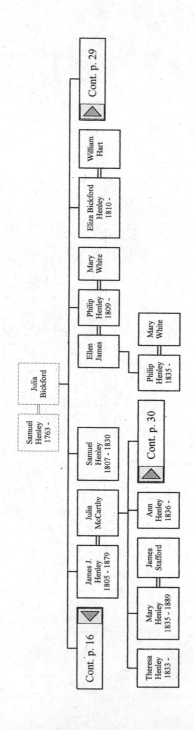

Chapter Seven (24 of 42)

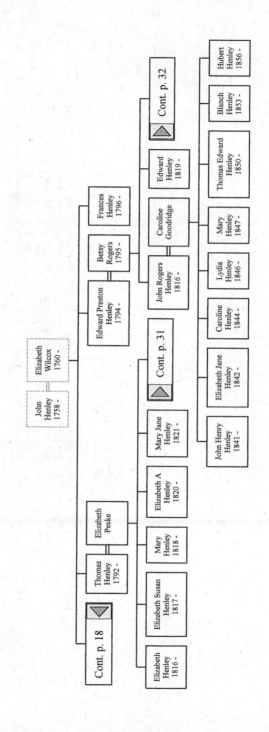

Chapter Seven (25 of 42)

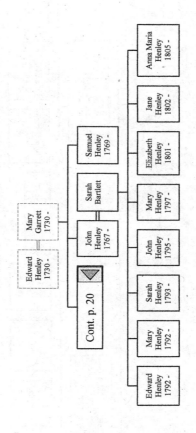

Cont. p. 20

Chapter Seven (26 of 42)

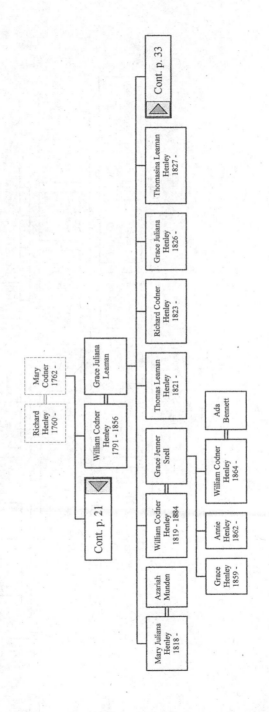

Cont. p. 33

Cont. p. 21

Richard Henley 1760 -

Mary Codner 1762 -

Grace Juliana Leaman

William Codner Henley 1791 - 1856

Mary Juliana Henley 1818 -

Azariah Munden

William Codner Henley 1819 - 1884

Grace Jenner Snell

Grace Henley 1859 -

Annie Henley 1862 -

William Codner Henley 1864 -

Ada Bennett

Thomas Leaman Henley 1821 -

Richard Codner Henley 1823 -

Grace Juliana Henley 1826 -

Thomasina Leaman Henley 1827 -

Chapter Seven (27 of 42)

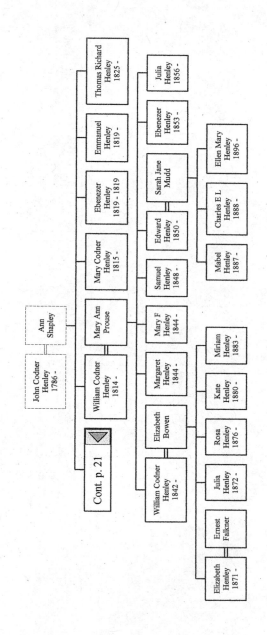

Cont. p. 21

Chapter Seven (28 of 42)

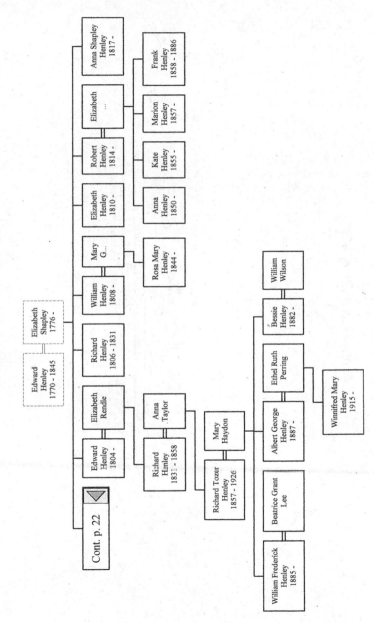

Cont. p. 22

Chapter Seven (29 of 42)

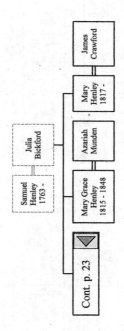

Chapter Seven (30 of 42)

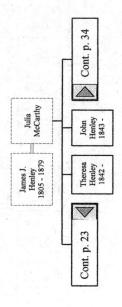

James J. Henley 1805 - 1879

Julia McCarthy

Theresa Henley 1842 -

Cont. p. 23

John Henley 1843 -

Cont. p. 34

Chapter Seven (31 of 42)

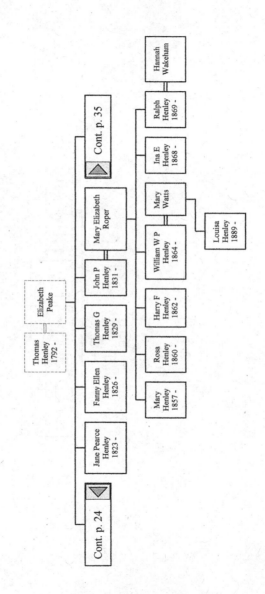

Cont. p. 24

Cont. p. 35

Thomas Henley 1792 -

Elizabeth Peake

Jane Pearce Henley 1823 -

Fanny Ellen Henley 1826 -

Thomas G Henley 1829 -

John P Henley 1831 -

Mary Elizabeth Roper

Mary Henley 1857 -

Rosa Henley 1860 -

Harry F Henley 1862 -

William W P Henley 1864 -

Mary Watts

Ina E Henley 1868 -

Ralph Henley 1869 -

Hannah Wakeham

Louisa Henley 1889 -

Chapter Seven (32 of 42)

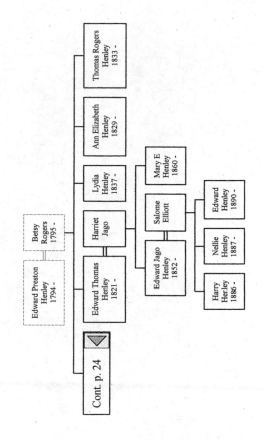

Chapter Seven (33 of 42)

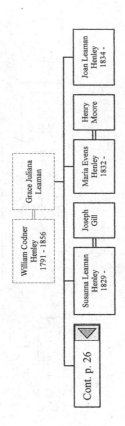

Cont. p. 26

Chapter Seven (34 of 42)

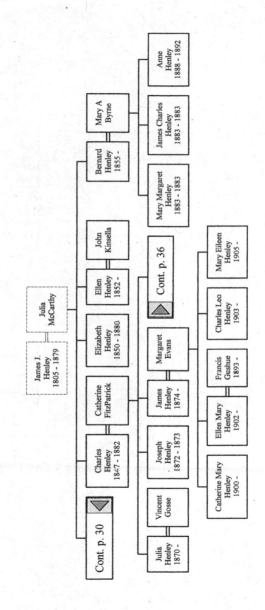

Chapter Seven (35 of 42)

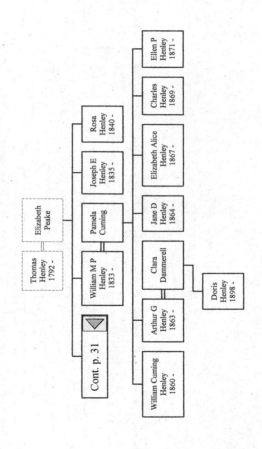

Cont. p. 31

Chapter Seven (36 of 42)

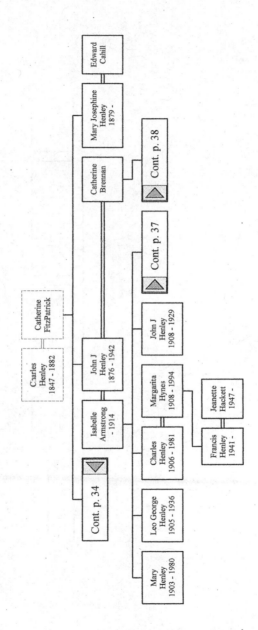

Cont. p. 38

Cont. p. 37

Cont. p. 34

Charles Henley 1847 - 1882

Catherine FitzPatrick

Mary Josephine Henley 1879 -

Edward Cahill

Catherine Brennan

John J Henley 1876 - 1942

Isabelle Armstrong - 1914

Mary Henley 1903 - 1980

Leo George Henley 1905 - 1936

Charles Henley 1906 - 1981

Margarita Hynes 1908 - 1994

John J Henley 1908 - 1929

Francis Henley 1941 -

Jeanette Hackett 1947 -

Chapter Seven (37 of 42)

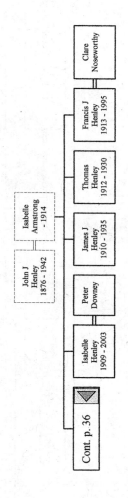

Cont. p. 36

Chapter Seven (38 of 42)

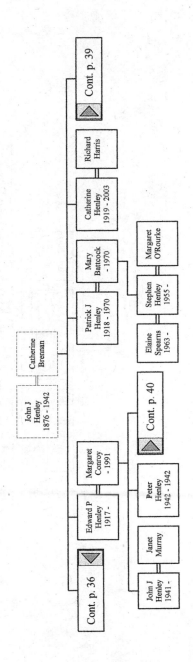

Cont. p. 39

Richard Harris

Catherine Henley 1919 - 2003

Mary Battcock - 1970

Margaret O'Rourke

Patrick J Henley 1918 - 1970

Stephen Henley 1955 -

Elaine Spearns 1963 -

John J Henley 1876 - 1942

Catherine Brennan

Cont. p. 40

Margaret Conroy - 1991

Edward P Henley 1917 -

Peter Henley 1942 - 1942

Janet Murray

Cont. p. 36

John J Henley 1941 -

Chapter Seven (39 of 42)

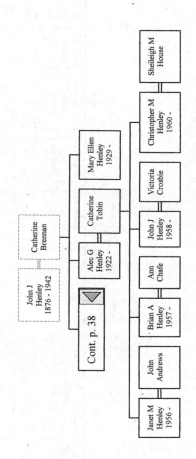

Cont. p. 38

Chapter Seven (40 of 42)

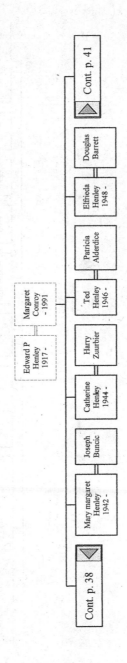

Cont. p. 41

Cont. p. 38

Chapter Seven (41 of 42)

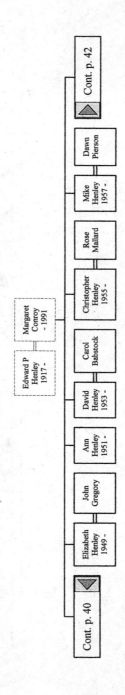

Cont. p. 40

Cont. p. 42

Chapter Seven (42 of 42)

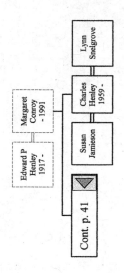

Cont. p. 41

Bibliography

Government Records

1. Great Britain:

Admiralty, Newfoundland series: vols. 470-71:1766-83.
Admiralty 1, North American series, vols. 480-82, 1745-66.
Colonial Office, series 42/1-5: Quebec 1763-66.
Colonial Office, series 194/13-35, 1706-1784, 1842, 1846-7.
Colonial Office, series 199/16, 1772-3.
County of Devon, Devon Parishes: Apprenticeship Indentures.
County of Devon, Devon Parishes: Land Tax Assessments, 1747/1832.
County of Devon: Inland Revenue Wills.
County of Devon, Quarter Sessions: Victuallers Recognizances.
Dartmouth: Dartmouth Borough Council, Minutes, 1783-1835.
House of Commons: Reports From The Committee On The State Of The Trade To Newfoundland, 1793.
War Office, series 1, In Letters and Papers, 1755-1800.
War Office, series 34, Amherst Papers, 1759- 77.

2. Newfoundland and Labrador:

City of St. John's: Council minutes 1902-9; Tax rolls, 1903-9.
Colonial Secretary, Voter's Lists:
    Brigus: 1869, 1889, 1893.
    Carbonear, 1832, 1835, 1839, 1844, 1848, 1849, 1855;
    Hr Grace: 1832, 1847, 1855, 1865, 1874, 1885;
Colonial Secretary, Outgoing correspondence, 1749-1815.
House of Assembly: Journals, 1833-92, 1904.
Registrar General, Registry of Vital Statistics: Registers of Births, marriages and deaths,

(Transcriptions), 1753/1891.
Registry of Deeds: Deeds and Wills, 1744-1859;
     Deeds, etc. vols. 29-60, 1905-1917.
Registry of Wills: Wills, 1824-1900.
Surrogate's Court: Minutes, Labrador 1810.
Supreme Court, St. John's: Pleas, 1798-1802.
Vice Admiralty Court: Labrador Court of Civil
     Jurisdiction, Minutes, 1826-33.

Private Records

1. Business:

Bird Papers: account books and correspondence
     of Joseph Bird, merchant of Newfoundland
     And Labrador, 1838-1844.
Hudson's Bay Company: Post records: North West
     River, Outward Corres, 1838-51 and Journals
     1836-51.
     London: Inward Corres, 1712-1816.
     Mingan: correspondence 1828-68.
     Montreal: correspondence, Inward 1825.
     Quebec: Inward Corres 1833-64.
     Rigolet: Journals, 1836-1870.
Lester, Benjamin, merchant, Trinity: Diaries,
     correspondence and ledgers, 1725-8,
     1761/1831.
Slade & Sons, Battle Harbour: ledgers and
     correspondence, 1794—1798.

2. Church:

England:

Abbots Bickington, 1614-1837.
Abbotsham, 1597-1734.
Abbotskerswell, 1607-1837.
Ashburton,
Ashprington, 1597-1811.
Axminster, -1800.
Berry Pomeroy, 1602-1909.
Bishopsteignton, 1653-1810.
Bovey Tracey, 1538-1837.
Bow, 1598-1801.

Brixham, 1556- 1801.
Broadhempston, 1681-1822.
Buckfastleigh, 1602-1837.
Chivelstone, 1684-1812.
Chudleigh Presbyterian/Independent, 1712-1815.
Churston, 1589-1837.
Cockington, 1628-1837.
Coffinswell, 1560-1837.
Combe-in-Teignhead, 1721-1810
Cornworthy, 1568-1837.
Countisbury, 1676-1757.
Dartington, 1538-1832.
Dartmouth St Petrox, 1610-1837.
Dartmouth St Saviour, 1586-1837.
Dartmouth Townstall, 1597-1837.
Dartmouth Independent 1727-1817.
Dartmouth St Nicholas, 1721-1837.
Dartmouth Presbyterian, 1726-1837.
Dawlish, 1609-1801.
Denbury, 1655-1810.
Dittisham, 1650-1837.
East Ogwell, 1663-1800.
Exeter, 1538-1837.
Ideford, 1598-1837.
Ipplepen, 1558-1837.
Kenton, 1694-1837.
Kingskerswell, 1606-1837.
Kingsteignton, 1670-1837.
Kingswear, 1608-1811.
Littleham, 1603-1812.
Little Hempston, 1544-1837.
Marshwood, 1614-1673.
Marldon, 1598-1812.
Martinhoe, 1633-1812.
Newton Abbot: Highweek, 1653-1814; Wolborough,
    1558-1805; Salem Independent, 1726-1837.
Paignton, 1559-1837.
Plymouth, 1581-1744.
Poole: Dissenting, 1760/1835.
    St James, 1653-1808.St James Anglican, 1722-
    47.
    Quaker, 1659/1820
    Unitarian, 1704/1782.
Ringmore, 1603-1811.

Ringmore by Kingsbridge, 1719-1814.
Salcombe, 1609-1837.
Shaldon, 1616-1812.
Slapton, 1606-1853.
Spreyton, 1760-66.
Staverton, 1556-1812.
Stokenham, 1574-1591.
Stoke Gabriel, 1539-1837.
Stoke Fleming, 1538-1837.
Stoke-in-Teignhead, 1538-1837.
Teigngrace, 1685-1837.
Teignmouth East, 1606-1805.
Teignmouth West, 1698-1805.
Torbryan, 1564-1810.
Torquay: St Marychurch, 1614-1837;
Churchwarden's Account Book, 1747-1827;
Tormoham, 1612-1812.
Totnes, 1556-1837.
Trentishoe, 1697-1812.
Uffculme, 1538-1837.
Werrington, 1654-1812.
Withycombe Raleigh, 1562-1812.

Newfoundland and Labrador:

Roman Catholic:

Carbonear: baptisms, 1849-65; marriages 1850-75.
Hr. Grace: baptisms, 1805-45, 1866; marriages,
    1805-45; 1866-72.
St. John's: Basilica of St. John the Baptist,
    parish registers, baptisms, 1837-
    92; marriages, 1793-1892.

Church of England:

Hr. Grace: baptisms and marriages, 1775-1830.
St. John's: Cathedral parish, baptisms and
    marriages, 1752-1836.

Congregational Church:

St. John's: baptisms 1780 -1861; marriages,
    1802-1850.

Methodist:

Brigus: baptisms and marriages, 1804-69.
  Burials, 1829-1837.
Carbonear, baptisms and marriages, 1793-1857.
Hr. Grace baptisms, 1775-1851; marriages 1776-
  1805.

3. Individuals:

Banks, Joseph, Journal of a voyage to
  Newfoundland and Labrador 1766.
Cartwright, Lieut. John, personal papers, 1773-
  1784.
Duff, Robert, Vice-Admiral: correspondence,
  1775, 1778-9.
Genealogical Society, St. John's, "Cemetery
  Transcriptions", Brigus United Church.
Graves, Thomas, Admiral: papers, 1761-1767.
Hole Family of Parke, Bovey Tracey, County of
  Devon: Family papers.
Legge, William, 2nd Earl of Dartmouth, Secretary
  Of State for the American department: papers,
  1688-1802.
McGillivray, Simon, Hudson's Bay Company Trader,
  Hamilton Inlet: papers, 1820-1.
McGrath, P T, Journalist, St. John's: papers,
  mainly a collection of historical material
  on the Labrador boundary case.
Murray Papers: papers of James Murray, 1759-
  1788.
Palk Family Papers: papers of the Palk family,
  landowners in Torquay, 18th and 19th centuries.
Perkins, Simeon, merchant and ship owner, Nova
  Scotia: Diaries, 1766-1812.
Richardson, William, Royal Navy Lieut: Journal
  of a voyage to Labrador, 1777.
Sharpe, Joshua: collection of papers regarding
  Labrador, 1764-9.
Shelburne, Lord: correspondence regarding
  Newfoundland trade, fishery and military
  Affairs, 1766-91.

Yorke family, Earls of Hardwicke: papers, 1754-73.

Published Works

1. Books/Booklets:

Cruwys, M.C.S, **The register of baptisms, marriages & burials of the parish of St. Andrew's, Plymouth, Co. Devon** (Exeter : Devon & Cornwall Record Society, 1954).

A Short History of Abbotskerswell (Abbotskerswell: Women's Institute, 1980).

Bardsley, Charles Wareing, **A Dictionary of English And Welsh Surnames** (Baltimore: Genealogical Publishing Company, 1968).

Barkham, Selma Huxley, **The Basque Coast of Newfoundland** (The Great Northern Peninsula Development Corporation, 1989).

Ibid, **Guipuzcoan Shipping in 1571 with particular reference to the decline of the transatlantic fishing industry** (Reno: Desert Research Institute, 1977).

Birnie, Arthur, **An Economic History of the British Isles** (London: Methuen & Co Ltd, 1969).

Bolton, J. L, **The Development of the English Economy To 1750** (London: Macdonald & Evans Ltd, 1971).

Born, Anne, **The Torbay Towns** (Chichester: Phillimore & Co Ltd, 1989).

Byrne, Cyril and Harry, Margaret, eds, **Talamh an Eisc: Canadian and Irish Essays** (Halifax: Nimbus, 1986).

Candow, James E and Carol Corbin, eds, **How deep is the ocean? : historical essays on Canada's Atlantic fishery** (Sydney, N S : University College of Cape Breton Press, 1997).

Cartwright, George, **A journal of transactions and events, during a residence of nearly sixteen years on the coast of Labrador, 3 vols.** (Newark: Allin and Ridge, 1792).

Carter, Philip, **Newton Abbot** (Exeter: The Mint Press, 2004).

Cell, Gillian T, **English enterprise in Newfoundland 1577-1660** (Toronto: University of Toronto Press, 1969).

Ibid, ed, **Newfoundland discovered: English attempts at colonization, 1610-1630** (London : Hakluyt Society, 1982.

Clodfelter, Michael, **Warfare and Armed Conflicts: A Statistical Reference to Casualty and Other Figures, 1500-2000.** 2nd edn. (London: McFarland & Company, Inc, 2002).

Cocks, Dr. John Somers, **Abbotskerswell** (Abbotskerswell: John Somers Cocks, 1995).

The Concise Dictionary of National Biography From Earliest Times to 1985, vol II (Oxford: Oxford University Press, 1992).

Coppock, J. T., **An Agricultural Geography of Great Britain** (London: G Bell & Sons, 1971).

Court, W. H. B, **A Concise Economic History of Britain From 1750 to Recent Times** (Cambridge: University Press, 1954).

Deane, Phyllis and Cole, W. A, **British Economic Growth 1688-1959** (Cambridge: University Press, 1964).

Drummond, J. C. and Wilbraham, Anne, **The Englishman's Food: A History of Five Centuries of English Diet** (London: Pimlico, 1994).

Duffy, Michael, et al, eds, **The New Maritime History of Devon**, vol 1 (Exeter: Conway Maritime Press, 1992).

Fischer, Lewis R and Eric Sager, eds, **The Enterprising Canadians: Entrepreneurs and Economic Development in Eastern Canada, 1820-1914** (St. John's: Maritime History Group, 1979).

Freeman, Ray, Dartmouth: **A New History of the Port And Its People** (Dartmouth: Harbour Books, 1983).

Ibid, **Changing Dartmouth: people and places** (Dartmouth: Harbour Books, 1984).

Gosling, W. G, **Labrador: Its Discovery,**

Exploration And Development (London: Alston Rivers, Ltd, 1910).

Goudie, Nina, **Down North on the Labrador circuit: the Court of Civil Jurisdiction, 1826 to 1833** (St. John's: Law Foundation of Newfoundland and Labrador, 2005).

Gray, Todd, ed, **Travels in Georgian Devon: The Illustrated Journals of the Reverend John Swete, 1789-1800**, vols. I, II (Exeter: Devon Books, 1997).

Guppy, Henry Brougham, **Homes of Family Names in Great Britain** (London: Harrison And Sons, 1890).

Handcock, W Gordon, **Soe longe as there comes noe women: Origins of English Settlement in Newfoundland** (St. John's: Breakwater Books, 1989).

Hanks, Patrick and Flavia Hodges, **A Dictionary of Surnames** (Oxford: Oxford University Press, 1989).

Harris, Michael, **Rare Ambition: The Crosbies Of Newfoundland** (Toronto: Penguin Books, 1993).

Harrison, Harry, **Surnames Of The United Kingdom: A Concise Etymological Dictionary** (Baltimore: Genealogical Publishing Company, 1969).

Head, C Grant, **Eighteenth century Newfoundland: a geographer's perspective** (Toronto : McClelland and Stewart, c.1976).

Havinden, M. A, **The South West And The Land** Exeter: University of Exeter, 1969).

Henley, Ellen Pamela, **William Cuming Henley: His Days And Ways** (Dartmouth: R Cranford & Son. 1953).

Henley, Frank, **Bright Memories: Being Reminiscences Of Frank Henley Containing An Account Of His Visits To Australia And New Zealand** (Torquay: W H Goss "Albion" Printing Works, 1887).

Hiller, James and Neary, Peter, eds. **Newfoundland in the Nineteenth and Twentieth Centuries: essays in interpretation** Toronto: University of Toronto Press, 1980).

Hoskins, W. G, **A New Survey Of England: Devon** (Newton Abbot: David & Charles, 1978).

Howard, A.J, **The Devon Protestation Returns 1641**, 2 vols. (Middlesex, N P, 1973).

Innis, Harold A, **The cod fisheries: the history of an international economy** (Toronto: University of Toronto Press, 1978).

Jones, Roger, **A Book Of Newton Abbot** (Bradford On Avon: Ex Libris Press, 1986).

Keir, David, **The Bowring Story** (London: Bodley Head Ltd, 1962).

Kennedy, John, **People of the Bays and Headlands: anthropological history and the fate of communities in the unknown Labrador** (Toronto: University of Toronto Press, 1995).

King, Linda, **The Life & Times of William Veale, Master Mariner 1791-1867** (Dartmouth: Dartmouth History Research Group, 1999).

King, Peter, **The Development of the English Economy To 1750** (London: Macdonald & Evans Ltd, 1971).

Laslett, Peter, **The World We Have Lost**, (London: Methuen and Company Limited, 1965).

Lounsbury, Ralph Greenlee, **The British Fishery at Newfoundland, 1637-1763** (New Haven: Yale University Press, 1934).

Lloyds Register of Shipping, 1764-1805.

Maclysaght, Edward, **The Surnames of Ireland, 3rd edn.** (Dublin: Irish Academic Press, 1978).

McDonald, Donna, **Lord Strathcona: A Biography of Donald Alexander Smith** (Toronto: Dundurn Press, 2002).

Mannion, John, ed, **The Peopling of Newfoundland: Essays in Historical Geography** (St. John's: Memorial University of Newfoundland 1977).

March, Edjar J, **Sailing Drifters: The Story of the Herring Luggers of England, Scotland and the Isle of Man** (London: Percival Marshall And Company Limited, 1952).

Marshall, William, **The Review And Abstract Of The County Reports To The Board Of Agriculture, vol 5: Southern and Peninsular** (York: Thomas Wilson & Sons, 1818).

Ibid, **The Rural Economy Of The West Of England, vol I** (London: G Nicol, 1796).

Ibid, **Rural Economy Of The West of England 1796,**

vol I (New York: Augustus M Kelley, 1970).

Mathias, Peter, **The First Industrial nation: An Economic History Of Britain, 1700-1914** (London: Methuen & Co Ltd, 1969).

Matthews, Keith, **Lectures on the history of Newfoundland, 1500**-1830 (St. John's: Breakwater Books, 1988).

Murphy, Brian, **A History of the British Economy, 1086-1970** (London: Longman Group Limited, 1973).

Newman, Peter C, **The Company of Adventurers** (Markham: Viking Press, 1985).

O'Flaherty, Patrick, **Old Newfoundland: A History to 1843** (St. John's: Long Beach Press, 1999).

Ibid, **Lost Country: The Rise and Fall of Newfoundland 1843-1933** (St. John's: Long Beach Press, 2005).

Ommer, Rosemary E, ed, **Merchant Credit and Labour Strategies in Historical Perspective** (Fredericton: Acadiensis Press, 1990).

Pope, Peter E, **Fish into wine: the Newfoundland plantation in the seventeenth century** (Chapel Hill: University of North Carolina Press, 2004).

Prowse, D W, **History of Newfoundland, 3rd edn.** (St. John's: Dicks And Company Limited, 1971).

Public Charities of the County of Devon (Exeter: The report of the Commissioners Concerning Charities, 1826).

Pulman, George P R, **The Book Of The Axe 4th edn,** (Bath: Kingmead reprints, 1969).

Reichel, Rev Oswald J, ed, **Devon Feet of Fines, Vol I, Richard I-Henry III** (Exeter: The Devon and Cornwall record Society, 1912).

The Report of the Commissioners Concerning Charities: Containing That part Which relates To the Country of Devon, vol II (Exeter: T Besley, 1828).

Ryan, Shannon, **Fish out of Water: The Newfoundland Saltfish Trade, 1814-1914** (St. John's: Breakwater Books 1986).

Sager, Eric W, Fischer, Lewis R and Pierson,

Stewart O, compilers, **Atlantic Canada and Confederation: Essays in Canadian Political Economy** (Toronto: University of Toronto Press, 1983).

Smallwood, Joseph Roberts and Pitt, Robert D W et al, eds, 5 vols. **Encyclopedia of Newfoundland and Labrador** (St John's: Newfoundland Book Publishers Limited and Harry Cuff Publications Limited, 1994).

Snow, Edward A, **A company history and financial statement as of Dec, 31, 1949,** (St. John's: James Baird (Labrador) Ltd, 1950).

Stephen, Sir Leslie and Lee, Sir Sidney, **The Dictionary Of National Biography From The Earliest Times To 1900, vol IX** (Oxford: Oxford University Press, 1993).

Stirling, Rev D.M, **A History of Newton Abbot and Newton Bushel** (Newton Abbot, 1830).

St Constantine Subsidy Rolls And Probate Calendars (Exeter: The Devon and Cornwall Record Society, 1910).

Stoate, T L, **Devon Taxes 1581-1660** (Bristol: T L Stoate, 1988).

Ibid, ed, **Devon Hearth Tax Return Lady Day 1674** (Bristol: T L Stoate, 1982).

Summers, Valerie A, **Regime Change In A Resource Economy: The Politics of Underdevelopment in Newfoundland 1825-1993** (St. John's: Memorial University, 1993).

Tapley-Soper, H, ed. and trans, **The register of baptisms, marriages & burials of the parish of Ottery St. Mary, Devon, 1601-1837,** 2 vols. (Exeter: The Devon and Cornwall Record Society, 1908-1929).

Ibid, **Parish of Topsham, co. Devon. : Marriages, baptisms & burials; A.D. 1600 to 1837. From the parochial register, the register of the independent meeting, the register of the Presbyterians, the register of the Quakers, together with copies of memorial inscriptions** (Exeter: Devon and Cornwall Record Society, 1938).

Vancouver, Charles, **General View of the Agriculture of the County of Devon** (Newton

Abbot: David & Charles Limited, 1808).

Vivian, Lieut. Col. J.L, **The Visitations of the County of Devon** (Exeter: Henry S Gland, 1895).

White J.T, **The History of Torquay** (Torquay: Directory Office, 1878).

White, William, **History, gazetteer and directory of Devonshire** (New York: A M Kelley, 1968).

Youings, Joyce, ed, **Devon Monastic Lands: Calendar Of Particulars For Grants 1536-1558,** (Torquay: Devon & Cornwall Record Society, 1955).

Zimmerly, David, **Cain's Land Revisited: Cultural Change in Central Labrador, 1775-1972** (St. John's: Institute of Social and Economic Research, Memorial University, 1975).

2. Computer Discs:

Census of England and Wales: Devon 1871 (Cinderford, Glou: Archive CD Books Ltd, 2004).

Crosbie, Gertrude, collector, **Births, Deaths and Marriages in Newfoundland Newspapers 1810-1890** (St. John's: Maritime History Archive, Memorial University, 2004).

British Isles Vital Records Index: England, Ireland, Scotland and Wales (Salt Lake City: The Church Of Jesus Christ Of Latter-day Saints, 1998).

1851 British Census: Devon Norfolk and Warwick (Salt Lake City: Church Of Jesus Christ Of Latter-Day Saints, 1997).

Northern Shipwrecks Database (Bedford: Northern Maritime Research, 2002).

Ships and Seafarers of Atlantic Canada (St. John's: Maritime History Archive, Memorial University, 1998).

3. Directories:

Gore's Liverpool Directory, 1825

Gore's Directory of Liverpool, 1827, 1829.

Gore's Directory of Liverpool and its Environs, 1853.

Hibbs, Richard, ed, **Who's Who In & From Newfoundland 1930** (St. John's: R Hibbs, 1930).

Hills, R, comp, **Might & Co's Directory of St. John's, Harbor Grace and Carbonear, Newfoundland, 1890** (Toronto: Might & Co, c.1891).

Holden's Annual Directory, Class First, 1st edn 1816-17 (London: Holden, c.1817).

Hutchinson, Thomas, **Newfoundland directory for 1864-65, containing alphabetical directories of each place in the colony, with a post office directory** (St. John's: T. McConnan, 1864).

Kent's Original London Directory, 1817.

Lovell's Newfoundland directory for 1871 :(London, ON: Genealogical Research Library, 1984).

McAlpine's Newfoundland directory: containing an alphabetical directory, and street directory of the city of St. John's and of the districts of the island ; also a complete classified business directory of Newfoundland, including the tariff of the colony. (Halifax, N.S.: McAlpine Publishing Company, 1898?).

McAlpine's Business Directory for St. John's 1904.

McAlpine's St. John's directory, 1908-1909: containing a directory of citizens and business and street directories: also directories of citizens of Harbor Grace and Carbonear and classified business firms of Newfoundland. (Halifax: McAlpine Publishing Co, 1908).

McAlpine's St. John's city directory, 1915: comprising a directory of St. John's, a classified business directory, a street directory and directory of Belle Isle, Carbonear and Harbor Grace. (Halifax: Royal Print & Litho, Ltd., 1915.

Mercantile Reference Book 1917 For The Dominion

Of Canada (Calgary: R G Dun & Co, 1917).
Pigot & Company's London & Provincial New
Commercial Directory For 1823-4.
Pigot & Company's Directory of Cheshire,
Cumberland, etc, 1828.
Pigot & Company's National Commercial Directory
of Cornwall, Dorsetshire, Devonshire,
Somersetshire & Wiltshire 1830.
Pigot's Directory, 1844 (London: I Slater,
1844).
Post Office London Directory 1846(London:
Michael Winton, 19914).
Rochforts 1885
Sharpe, John, comp, Directory for the Towns of
St. John's, Harbour Grace & Carbonear,
Newfoundland for 1885-86 (St. John's: N P,
1885)
Slater's Directory of Important English Towns,
1847.
Slater's Directory of Gloucestershire,
Monmouthshire, etc, 1859.
Triennial Directory of London, Westminster,
Southwark And Ten Miles Distant for 1817-19.
The Universal British Directory, 1793-1798.
West of England Pocket Book or Gentleman's
Diary With An Almanac, 1853.
West of England And Trewman's Exeter Pocket
Journal or Gentleman's Diary, With An
Almanac, 1858. (Exeter: Henry Besley, 1858).

4. Newspapers and Periodicals:

The Daily News, St. John's, 1903.
Devon & Cornwall Notes & Queries, (Exeter:
James G Commin, 1931).
The Devonshire Association for the Advancement
of Science, Literature and Art, vol XCV.
The Evening Telegram, St. John's, 1903.
Gentleman's Magazine, 1856, 1859.
The London Gazette, 1752-1979.
The Newfoundland Quarterly, St. John's, 1902-
1977.
Public Ledger, St. John's, 1831.
Transactions of the Devonshire Association,

vols. 10, 31, 33, 83, 125. (Highweek, Newton
Abbot).
The Weekly Herald And Conception Bay General
Advertiser, Hr Grace, 1845-50.

Unpublished Works

1. Theses/Dissertations/Papers/Transcriptions:

Boyd's Marriage Index for Devon 1538-1837, 25
vols. (Exeter: The Devon and Cornwall Record
Society, 1932)
Bradley, David Gordon, "Smugglers, Schemers,
Scoundrels And Sleeveens: An Analysis of
Merchant-Client Relations At Bonavista,
Newfoundland, 1875-1895" (St. John's:
Memorial University, M A Thesis, 1994).
"Calendar of Deeds and Documents in Exeter City
Library" (Exeter: Devon Record Office).
Chang, Margaret, "Newfoundland in Transition:
the Newfoundland trade and Robert Newman and
Company, 1780-1805" (St. John's: Memorial
University, M A Thesis, 1974).
The Devon and Cornwall Record Society, "Family
Files", (Exeter: Westcountry Studies Library)
Devon and Cornwall Record Society, Exeter,
"Marriage Licences 1523-1762", 4 vols.
(Exeter, 1947).
The Devon Family History Society "Family Files",
(Exeter: Devon Family History Society).)
Earle, Lucy M, "Like a cat would watch a rat :
social and economic relationships between
Baine, Johnston & Company Ltd., and the
fishermen of the Battle Harbour district,
1940-1945" (Memorial University, Honors
Dissertation, 2003).
Edwards, L W Lawson, transcriber, "Devon
Nonconformist Registers" vol. 1.
Fursdon C.A.T., transcriber, "Devon Marriage
Licences, 1734-1827", 11 vols. (Exeter: The
Devon and Cornwall Record Society, 1939).
Fursdon, A. A, "Marriage Indexes for Exeter",
Vols. 1-9, 1558-1837 (Exeter: The Devon and
Cornwall Record Society, 1976).

Ibid, "Marriage Allegations, Devon and Cornwall 1720-1725", vol 4. (Exeter: The Devon and Cornwall Record Society, 1931).

Hiller, James, "The foundation and the early years of the Moravian mission in Labrador, 1752-1805" (St. John's: Memorial University, M A Thesis, 1967).

Ibid, "A History of Newfoundland, 1874-1901" (Cambridge: University of Cambridge, Ph. D Thesis, 1971).

Howard, Mrs. Mildred, "Howard Collection: A Collection of Births, Deaths and Marriages in Newfoundland Newspapers", 6 vols, 1810-1873.

Joy, John Lawrence, "The Growth and Development Of Trades And Manufacturing In St. John's 1870-1914" (St. John's: Memorial University, M A Thesis, 1977).

Lee, Mac, "Miscellaneous collection of historical material on Hr Grace and Conception Bay, 1770/1965".

Matthews, Keith, "A History of the West of England-Newfoundland Fishery" (Oxford: University of Oxford, Ph. D thesis, 1968).

Matthews, Keith, "Name Files" (St. John's: Maritime History Archive).

Matthews, Keith: Fonds, series 4, Sub-series 4.36: "Admirals Log Books, 1763-1779".

Niering, Francis Eduard, "Andrew Pinson: Dartmouth Merchant, ship owner and gentleman farmer trading to Labrador" (Exeter: University of Exeter, M A Thesis, 1999).

Northway, A. M, The Devon Fishing Industry 1760-1860 (Exeter: University of Exeter, M A Thesis, 1969).

Orr, J A, "Scottish Merchants in the Newfoundland Trade, 1800-1835: A Colonial Community in Transition" (St. John's: Memorial University, M A Thesis, 1987).

Rowe, Margery M and Andrew M Jackson, eds, "Exeter Freemen 1266-1967" (Exeter: The Devon and Cornwall Record Society, 1973).

Smith, Mrs. G H, transcriber, "Parish register of Wolborough" (Newton Abbot: The Devon and

Cornwall Record Society, 1958).)

Smith, Marjorie, "Newfoundland 1815-1840: A Study of Merchantocracy" (St. John's: Memorial University, M A Thesis, 1968).

Warr, Donald A, "A study of Newman's Company in Newfoundland from 1850-1859" (Memorial University: a paper presented to the Maritime History Group, 1973).

Wood, Herbert, trans, "Tormoham (Torquay) Parish Register 1637-1743" (Exeter: 1941).

Index of Places and Persons (other than Henley)

Abbotskerswell, Devon, 5,31-2, 68-70, 72-3, 77-9, 95, 99, 101-3, 106-10, 112-15, 119, 124-5, 128, 135-41, 143-4, 153, 163-4.

Adams, Joan, Dartmouth, Devon, 128, 171.

Aillik, Labrador, 66.

Albany River, On, 45.

Amsterdam, Holland, 74.

Antelope Tickle, Labrador, 53.

Armstrong, Isabelle, St. John's, NL, 155, 201.

Arnell, Emelinge, Paignton, Devon, 135.

Ashburton, Devon, 77.

Australia, 147-8.

Backaller, Susan, Thornley, Devon, 143, 186.

Bad Bay, Labrador, 53.

Bailey, Mary, Brixham, Devon, 128, 171.

Baird, James, Labrador, 8.

Baker, William, Stokeinteignhead, Devon, 173.

Bartlett, Sarah, Newton Abbot, Devon, 121, 190.

Battcock, Mary, St. John's NL, 157, 203.

Bay Roberts, Newfoundland, 38, 141.

Beard & Co, Dartmouth, Devon, 55.

Beard & Hunt, Dartmouth, Devon, 43, 56.

Beard, Nancy, Dartmouth, Devon, 131, 174.

Beard, Phillip, Dartmouth, Devon, 54-5, 57.

Belle Isle, NL, 42, 48, 51, 53.

Bennett, Ada, Essex, 140, 191.

Berry, Alice, Chudleigh, Devon, 105-6, 127, 173.

Berry Pomeroy, Devon, 131.

Bickford, Barbara, Abbotskerswell, Devon, 166.

Bickford, Julia, Wolborough, Devon, 141, 150-1, 181.

Bickford, Susanna,

Torquay, Devon, 135, 184.

Bird, Joseph, Dorset, 10, 64.

Bishopsteignton, Devon 105,127.

Black Islands, Labrador, 62.

Blagdon, Devon, 73, 77.

Blake, Mary, Totnes, Devon, 144, 181.

Bond, George, Bishopsteignton, Devon, 105.

Bond, George, Stokeinteignhead, Devon, 127.

Bond, John, Kingskerswell, Devon, 31.

Bond, Robert, St. John's, NL, 31.

Bond, William, Kingsbridge, Devon, 73.

Boston, MA, 83.

Bow, Devon, 96.

Bowden, Mary, West Teignmouth, Devon, 105, 127, 173.

Bowen Elizabeth, Bristol, 142, 192.

Bovey Tracey, Devon, 70.

Brennan, Catherine Ellen, St. John's, NL, 155, 201.

Brigus, NL, 140-1, 154.

Bristol, England, 28, 42, 75, 142

Brixham, Devon, 19, 99, 125, 127-8, 132.

Broadclyst, Devon, 75, 149.

Brooking, Mary, Dartmouth, Devon, 55.

Bulley, Job & Cross, St. John's, NL, 31, 121.

Burton, George, St. John's, NL, 36, 37, 120.

Butler, Mary, St. John's, NL, 165.

Byrne, Mary Ann, St. John's, NL, 154, 199. 83, 101, 136, 150-4.

Cahill, Edward, St. John's, NL, 155, 201.

Cape Broyle, NL, 119.

Carbonear, NL, 34, 38, 67, 83, 101, 136, 150-4.

Carroll, Daniel, St. John's, NL, 155.

Cartwright, George, 41.

Cartwright, Labrador, 59, 65.

Cecil, William, London, 22.

Channel, George, Dartmouth, Devon, 171.

Chateaux Bay, Labrador, 40, 44, 48, 53, 57, 59-60.

Cholwich Family, Blackawton, Devon, 55, 57.

Chudleigh, Devon, 46, 105-6, 125-7, 136.

Churchwell, Ann, Abbotskerswell, Devon, 108, 112-3, 115, 118, 144, 172.

Churston Ferrers, Devon, 105.

Clark, A C & Co Limited, Bristol, 75.

Coaker, William, St. John's, NL, 7.

Cocks, Dr John Somers, Abbotskerswell, Devon, 137, 214.

Codners, Kingskerswell, Devon, 31-2.

Codner, John, Abbotskerswell, Devon, 70.

Codner, Mary, Abbotskerswell, Devon, 70, 114-5, 136, 164-5, 179.

Codner, Richard, Abbotskerswell, Devon, 138.

Codner, Richard, Torquay, Devon, 36,137.

Codners, Torquay, Devon, 138.

Colcock, William Henry, Bristol, 75.

Cole, Mary, Churston, Devon, 105, 125-6, 135,

Conche, NL, 53.

Conroy, Margaret, St. John's, NL, 203.

Crawford, James, Carbonear, NL, 153, 194.

Creed, Jane, Kingskerswell Devon, 117, 119, 182.

Creed, Joan, Kingskerswell Devon, 121, 185.

Crosbie family, NL, 7.

Croydon, Surrey, 140-1.

Cuming, Pamela, Dartmouth, Devon, 133, 200.

Curyer, Ann, Abbotskerswell, Devon, 106, 169.

Dammerell, Clara, Dartmouth, Devon, 134, 200.

Dartmouth, Devon, 5, 22, 28, 31-2, 53, 55, 57-8, 93, 100-1, 107-8, 110-12, 116, 120, 123, 125, 128, 130-4.

Davis, Henry, West Teignmouth, Devon, 126.

Davis Inlet, Labrador, 66.

Davis, Mary, Newton Abbot, Devon, 123, 185.

Daymond, Joseph, St. John's, 83.

Dever, Agnes, Berry Pomeroy, Devon, 131, 174.

Devonport, Devon, 118, 134.

Divers Island, Labrador, 59.

Dolus, Joseph, Chudleigh, Devon, 126.

Downey, Peter, Fort Pepperell, NL, 156, 202.

Drachart, Rev, Labrador, 42.

Duders, St Marychurch, Devon, 32.

Dumpling Island, Labrador, 58-9, 61-3.

Earle, Louisa, South Zeal, Devon, 143, 186.

East Ogwell, Devon, 119.

Edwards, Richard, Governor, 116.

Elliott, Salome, Brixham, Devon, 132, 197.

Endell, Thomas, Teigngrace, Devon, 172.

Erven Agnes, Abbotskerswell, Devon, 101, 103, 166.

Esquimaux Bay, Labrador, 48, 59, 67.

Exeter, Devon, 10, 15-16, 18, 31, 42, 45-6, 94-5, 101- 02, 111-12, 115, 121, 125, 143, 165.

Exmouth, Devon, 19.
Evans, Margaret. St. John's,
NL, 155, 199.
Falkner, Ernest, London,
143, 192.
Farley & Henley, Newton
Abbot, Devon, 37.
Ferryland, NL, 55, 153.
Fitzpatrick, Catherine, St.
John's, 154, 199.
Fogo, NL, 13.
Fogwill, John, Berry Pomeroy,
Devon, 181.
Fogwill, William, Berry
Pomeroy, Devon, 181.
Forteaux, Labrador, 44.
Fox, Elizabeth, St.
Marychurch, Devon, 144, 175.
Fox Harbour, Labrador, 53.
Fry, Susanna, St. John's, NL,
151.
Furneaux, George, Brixham,
Devon, 132, 183.
Furse, Mary, St. Marychurch,
Devon, 135, 173.
Garret, Mary,
Abbotskerswell, Devon, 118-
9, 123, 179.
Gill, Joseph, Wiltshire, 198.
Gloucester, MA, 74, 155.
Goodenough, Nicholas,
Highweek, Devon, 136, 184.
Goodridge, A F, St.
John's, NL, 31.
Goodridge, Caroline,
Dartmouth, Devon, 132,
189.
Goodridge family, Devon
and NL, 32, 62.
Gosse, Vincent, St.
John's, NL, 155, 199.
Grady, Labrador, 59, 67.
Graham, Aaron, St.
John's, NL, 116.
Green Bay, Labrador, 53.
Guernsey, 118.
Gushue, Francis, St.
John's, NL, 199.
Guy, John, Bristol, 28.
Hamer, James, Exeter,
Devon, 143, 186.
Hamlyn, William, St.
Marychurch, Devon, 187.
Hannaford, John,
Abbotskerswell, Devon, 184.

Harbour Grace, NL, 38,
141, 153-4.
Harris, Richard, St.
John's, NL, 157, 203.
Hart, William,
Kingskerswell, Devon,
153, 181, 188.
Haven, Rev, Labrador, 42.
Hawkes, Rev. P, Torquay,
Devon, 147.
Haydon, Mary, London, 149,
193.
Henley Harbour, Labrador,
1-3, 39, 41, 43-5, 51-2,
56, 59-60.
Henley Island, Labrador,
41, 43-4.
Herring Neck, NL, 7.
Hickman, A E, St. john's,
NL, 8.
Highweek, Devon, 104, 114,
126, 136-7, 151, 165.
Hill, Rev, Labrador, 42.
Hillingdon, Middlesex,
143.
Hine: Pinson & Hine, 43,
54-7.
Holdsworth family, Devon
and NL, 32, 55, 57.
Hoop-Pole Cove, Labrador,
53.
Hoyles, Hugh, St. John's,
NL, 31.
Hoyles, Newman, Dartmouth,
Devon, 31-2.
Hull, Port of, England,
20.
Hunt family, Dartmouth,
Devon, 39-41, 43, 53-9,
61-6, 130-1.
Huntingdon, Labrador, 62.
Hyett, William, Newton
Abbot, Devon, 175.
Hynes, Margarita, St.
John's, NL, 201.
Innis, Harold, historian,
20, 48.
Ipplepen, Devon, 16, 76.
Isle of Spears, Labrador,
33-4.
Jago, Harriet, Dartmouth,
NL, 132, 197.
James, Ellen, Carbonear,
NL, 152, 188.

Jardine, John, Newton Abbot,
 Devon, 37, 122.
Jardine, Margaret, Newton
 Abbot, Devon, 122, 185.
Job, John, St. John's, NL, 32.
Kew, England, 13, 15.
Kingsbridge, Devon, 73.
Kingskerswell, Devon, 31-2,
 113, 115, 117, 119, 153.
Kinsella, John, St. John's, NL,
 154, 199.
Kolbec, Nova Scotia, 153.
Lambert, Maria, Ashburton,
 Devon, 103, 166.
Lance Cove, Labrador, 53.
L'Anse Aux Meadows, Labrador,
 47.
Lang, Ann, St. Marychurch,
 Devon, 144, 175.
Lang, William,
 Stokeinteignhead, Devon, 126.
Lannon, Jane, Dartmouth, Devon,
 129, 174.
Laslett, Peter, social
 scientist, 68.
Leaman, Grace Juliana, Torquay,
 Devon, 140, 191.
Leaman, Thomas, Torquay, Devon
 and Croydon, Surrey, 141.
Ledbury, Hereford, 74.
Lee, Beatrice, Torquay, Devon,
 193.
Lindfield, Sussex, 121.
Liverpool, England, 64, 153.
London, England, 26, 38,
 42, 54, 62, 64, 67, 72-4,
 77-8, 121, 123, 133, 139,
 140-3, 149, 151.
London, ON, 157.
Long Island, Labrador, 59,
 67.
Lyons, France, 74.
MacDonald, John A, Ottawa,
 81.
MacMuldrow, W G P, South
 Africa, 153, 164-5.
McCarthy, Julia, Harbour
 Grace, NL, 154, 188.
McDuerog, John, Kingswear,
 Devon, 134.
McGrath, P T, St. John's,
 43, 130.
Martin, Mary,
 Stokeinteignhead, Devon,
 105, 127, 173.

Martyne, Jane,
 Abbotskerswell, Devon,
 106, 172.
Mary's Harbour, Labrador,
 3, 53.
Matthews, Keith,
 historian, 22, 25-7.
Mecatina, Labrador, 48.
Melbourne, Australia, 16,
 148.
Mends, Ann, Plymouth,
 Devon, 131, 174.
Miller, John,
 Abbotskerswell, Devon,
 179.
Milne, Capt, British Navy,
 61.
Moore, Henry T, Harbour
 Grace, NL, 141, 198.
Moore, Joan, St.John's,
 117, 182.
Moretonhampstead, Devon,
 149.
Morris, E P, St. John's,
 NL, 80.
Moxey, Francis, Brixham,
 Devon, 127.
Mudd, Sarah Jane,
 Nantwich, Cheshire
 142,192.
Mudge, John, St.
 Marychurch, Devon, 180.
Munden, Azariah, Brigus,
 NL, 140-1, 154, 191, 194.
Munden, Mary Grace,
 Brigus, NL, 151-2
Munn, W A, St. John's, NL,
 153.
Murray, Governor, Quebec,
 42-3.
Mussey, Elizabeth,
 Churston, Devon, 126.
Newman family, Dartmouth
 and NL, 8, 13, 32, 55.
Newman, Sir Robert
 William, Dartmouth,
 Devon, 55.
Newton Abbot, Devon, 5,
 32, 35, 37, 69, 70, 73-7,
 93-4, 98-106, 108, 110,
 113-15, 117-19, 121-5,
 131, 135-7, 142, 150-1.
Newton Bushel, Devon, 94,
 120.
New Zealand, 147.

Niger River, Labrador, 53.
Noble & Hunt, 54-5.
Noble, John, Dartmouth,
  Devon, 116.
Noble & Pinson, 32, 41, 43-4,
  52-4, 56.
North River, NL, 156.
North Tawton, Devon, 143.
North West River, Labrador, 66.
Norwood, Surrey, 121.
Noseworthy, Clare, Pouch
  Cove, NL, 157, 202.
Osborne, Marie, Abbotskerswell,
  Devon, 106, 166.
Ottawa, Ontario, 14-16, 45.
Oxenham, Alice: see Oxneham.
Oxneham, Alice,
  Abbotskerswell, Devon, 113,
  172.
Palk, Sir Laurence, Torquay,
  Devon, 145.
Palliser, Governor Hugh, 39-40,
  42.
Paris, France, 74.
Parnell, John, Totnes,
  Devon, 132-3.
Pater, Joanne, St.
  Marychurch, Devon, 144, 175.
Peake, Elizabeth, Dartmouth,
  Devon, 132-3, 189.
Penge, London, 143.
Periam, Margarette,
  Exeter, Devon, 101.
Perring, Ethel, Torquay,
  Devon, 149, 193.
Petherbridge, William,
  Dartmouth, Devon, 129,
  178.
Pinhoe, Devon, 73, 77.
Pinson, Andrew, Dartmouth,
  Devon, 32.
Pitt's Harbour, Labrador,
  41.
Plymouth, Devon, 16, 18,
  119, 131.
Preston, Grace, Dartmouth,
  Devon, 129, 174.
Prosser, James, Dartmouth,
  Devon, 171.
Prouse, Mary Ann, Torquay,
  Devon, 142, 192.
Prowse, D W, St. John's,
  NL, 21, 29, 30, 42.
Paignton, Devon, 31-2, 73,
  77, 103, 135, 142.

Paradise, Labrador, 59.
Quebec, CA, 43, 45, 48-9,
  54.
Rendell family, Ringmore,
  Devon, 32.
Rendle, Elizabeth,
  Torquay, Devon, 148, 193.
Renews, NL, 32, 37, 136-7,
  150, 152.
Rhodes, see Roads.
Rigolet, Labrador, 64.
Ringmore, Devon, 32, 121.
River Phillip, Nova
  Scotia, 153.
Roads, Mary, Dartmouth,
  Devon, 107, 110, 125,
  169.
Rodd, Mary,
  Abbotskerswell, Devon,
  114-5, 135, 179.
Rodway, Bertram,
  Middlesex, 133.
Rogers, Betsy, Dartmouth,
  Devon, 132, 189.
Rolls, Mary,
  Abbotskerswell, Devon,
  172.
Roper, Mary, Dartmouth,
  Devon, 134, 196.
Round I, Labrador, 59.
Row family, Torquay,
  Devon: see Stabb, Row and
  Holmwood.
Ryan, William, St. John's,
  NL, 37
St. John's, NL, 2, 4, 6,
  7, 13, 15-6, 31-40, 51,
  55, 61, 72, 80, 82-4, 86-
  9, 93, 95, 99,100-1, 108,
  115-22, 130-1, 136, 150-
  1; 153-5, 157-8, 160,
  165.
Sandhurst, Australia, 148.
Sandwich Bay, Labrador,
  55-7, 61-2, 64, 67.
Schloerer, Rev, Labrador,
  42.
Seal Islands, Labrador,
  53.
Shapley, Ann, Torquay,
  Devon, 142, 186.
Shapley, Elizabeth, St.
  Marychurch, Devon, 144-5,
  148, 164-5.
Shapley, Mary, Torquay,

Devon, 144, 164, 181.
Shepheard, John, Plymouth,
  Devon, 131.
Shere, John, Abbotskerswell,
  Devon, 70.
Slade & Sons, Fogo and
  Battle Hr, NL, 13, 41.
Smith, Donald, HBC, 66.
Snell, Grace Jenner, Croydon,
  Surrey, 140, 191.
Stabb, Row and
  Holmwood, St. John's, NL,
  32.
Stafford, James, St. John's,
  NL, 2, 154, 188.
Stokeinteignhead, Devon, 105,
  126-7.
Studdy, Margaret, Teigngrace,
  Devon, 106, 172.
Taylor, Anna, Melbourne,
  Australia, 193.
Taylor, James, North Tawton,
  143, 186.
Teigngrace, Devon, 106.
Thorne, Dunes, Wolborough,
  Devon, 104, 170.
Tobin, Catherine, St. John's,
  NL, 160, 204.
Tomlin, Mary, London, 143.
Totnes, 31, 77, 123, 132,
  134, 144.
Venning, Elizabeth,
  Exeter, Devon, 102, 115,
  175.
Wakeham, Hannah,
  Dartmouth, Devon, 134,
  196.
Watts, Mary, Totnes,
  Devon, 134, 196.
White, Mary, Carbonear,
  NL, 152, 188.
Wilcox, Elizabeth,
  Dartmouth, Devon, 132,
  183.
Wills, Mary, Newton Abbot,
  Devon, 104, 126, 170.
Wills, Robert,
  Abbotskerswell, Devon,
  169.
Wilson, William, Torquay,
  Devon, 149, 193.
Wittecer, Willmet, Dartmouth,
  Devon, 128, 171.
Yabsley, Peter,

Kingskerswell, Devon,
113, 115, 182.